9/29/11
$89.95

EXPLORING THE *BHAGAVAD GĪTĀ*

This is potentially one of the most significant books to emerge in recent times on how to read the Gītā, *for it provides a clear way forward to make coherent sense of one of the most important yet methodologically intractable texts of religious Hinduism. I found this book an illumining experience.*

Julius Lipner FBA, Professor of Hinduism and the Comparative Study of Religion and Fellow of Clare Hall, University of Cambridge, UK

A fascinating book which throws new light on the Gītā, *and should help to make it more accessible to those who wish to read this great spiritual classic.*

Keith Ward FBA, Regius Professor of Divinity Emeritus and Fellow of Christ Church College, University of Oxford, UK

Ithamar Theodor approaches the ancient Bhavadad Gītā *with a modern mind and finds much in it that deserves our attention. Locating his study within Comparative Theology and identifying the various layers of meaning in the text will help those unacquainted with it to find their way through this complex classic. Combining the philosophical-theoretical with the ethical-practical the author shows the universal relevance of the* Gītā*'s teaching. Since Sarvepalli Radhakrishnan nobody has offered as penetrating a study of this classic as Ithamar Theodor has done.*

Klaus Klostermaier FRSC, Distinguished Professor of Hinduism and Religious Studies Emeritus, University of Manitoba, Canada

For my beloved daughters;
Inbal Jāhnavī, Nili Nīla Mādhava devī and Kamah Kamalinī

Exploring the *Bhagavad Gītā*

Philosophy, Structure and Meaning

ITHAMAR THEODOR
University of Haifa, Israel

ASHGATE

Published by
Ashgate Publishing Limited
Wey Court East
Union Road
Farnham
Surrey, GU9 7PT
England

Ashgate Publishing Company
Suite 420
101 Cherry Street
Burlington
VT 05401-4405
USA

www.ashgate.com

British Library Cataloguing in Publication Data
Theodor, Ithamar, 1959–
Exploring the Bhagavad gita: philosophy, structure and meaning.
1. Bhagavadgita – Criticism, interpretation, etc.
I. Title
294.5'924046–dc22

Library of Congress Cataloging-in-Publication Data
Theodor, Ithamar, 1959–
Exploring the Bhagavad Gita: philosophy, structure, and meaning / Ithamar Theodor.
p. cm.
Includes bibliographical references and index.
ISBN 978-0-7546-6658-5 (hardcover: alk. paper) – ISBN 978-1-4094-0260-2 (ebook)
1. Bhagavadgita – Criticism, interpretation, etc. I. Title.
BL1138.66.T48 2009
294.5'924046--dc22

2009040967

ISBN 9780754666585 (hbk)
ISBN 9781409402602 (ebk)

Mixed Sources
Product group from well-managed forests and other controlled sources
www.fsc.org Cert no. SA-COC-1565
© 1996 Forest Stewardship Council
FSC

Printed and bound in Great Britain by
MPG Books Group, UK

Contents

Pronunciation Guide

For readers unfamiliar with the subtleties of the Sanskrit alphabet and the commonly accepted transliteration system, a very brief guide is offered, roughly exemplifying the pronunciation of the main transliterated characters:

ā, ī,: *gītā*	geetaa
ū: *sūtra*	sootra
ai, ś: *vaiśya*	vayshya
au, ī: Draupadī	Drowpadee
ṣ, ṭ, ā, ṅ: *aṣṭāṅga*	ashtaanga
ṇ, ḍ: *pāṇḍava*	paandava
ṛ, ṣ, ṇ: Kṛṣṇa	Krishna
c, ā: Cekitāna	Chekitaana
jñ: *jñāna*	gyaana
ṇ: *Karṇa*	Karna
ś: Aśvins	Ashvins
ṁ: *ahaṁkāra*	ahankaara (the *ṁ* may be in most cases translated into *n* but before *p*, *ph*, *b* and *bh* into *m*)

Preface

There are various possible ways of reading the *Bhagavad Gītā*; it can be read as a work of literature or poetry, it can be read as a work in the realm of Indology and examined from the point of view of Oriental studies, and it can otherwise be read as a work of philosophy or theology. As a work of literature or poetry, its literary and poetical aspects would naturally be highlighted; as such, the verses' meters, the particular epithets of Arjuna and Kṛṣṇa and the corresponding emotions evoked by their application – these and similar aspects will possibly be looked into. As a work of Indology, its historical and linguistic aspects would be highlighted and, as such, questions regarding the date of its compilation, the singularity or plurality of authors, the linguistic structure of the text, and its relation to the context of the *Mahābhārata* would be naturally considered. As a work of philosophy or theology, its conceptual structure, its underlying assumptions and its prevailing ideas would be mainly considered and examined, and this is the thrust of the present edition. *Bhagavad Gītā* scholarship has become somewhat complicated and sophisticated, so much so that, at times, a gap has appeared, distancing the general readership from the scholarly analysis of this widely read text. The present work is perhaps driven by a pedagogical impulse and, as such, has not only a different mood than the analytical approach, but different aims; as far as the mood, I invite the readers to relax, to enter into a somewhat contemplative mood as befitting the reading of a great classical treatise. As far as the aims, I hope to further the reading of the *Bhagavad Gītā* as a work in the realm of philosophy or theology, and to help the reader gain a vision or a *darśana* of this great treatise. For this reason I am consciously avoiding a comprehensive bibliography and dense footnotes, as these may distract the reader from the simple but deep ideas originally conveyed.

The present work was born as a work of theology, and was sharpened and further articulated in the milieu of the Theology Faculty, University of Oxford. One of its main aims is to offer a unifying structure, open to a rational examination, a structure which will tie the text together. This structure is constructed applying the metaphor of a 'three-storey house' and it is mainly composed of two components; on the one hand, there are three different storeys or floors, and on the other hand, a staircase leading the house's residents from the first floor towards the second and third floors. The three floors represent three levels of reality, whereas the staircase represents a transformational ladder of ethical and spiritual refinement. In the wider sense, I would like this work to be considered a contribution not only to the study of the *Bhagavad Gītā*, but to the emerging field of Comparative Theology, as once the structures of great theological works could be articulated, these could be compared, contrasted and grouped together, thereby offering a unified sense of pluralistic spirituality which may serve as an alternative to materialism. Originally,

Greek philosophy was inseparable from Greek religion, and only gradually was it articulated as a universal philosophy. Similarly, this work may further a slight step in this direction, in that it emphasizes the *Bhagavad Gītā*'s philosophical nature, relevant also in a non-Hindu context. Examining many of the available academic editions, one realizes that they offer an introduction followed by a verse translation; the present edition joins the few editions which render the text divided into sections, and add a commentary; I hope that this approach proves to be useful. Let me conclude by quoting the *Bhagavad Gītā* itself:

> This is a royal science, a royal mystery, the supreme purifier, experienced directly, it conforms to *dharma*, pleasant to act upon and eternal.[1]

May the readers enjoy this great treatise.

Ithamar Theodor

Clare Hall and the Divinity Faculty
University of Cambridge, January 3rd, 2008

[1] *BG* 9.2.

Acknowledgements

It is a great pleasure to reflect upon the long route the composition of this work has taken, and to acknowledge with deep gratitude the teachers, scholars, students, friends and relatives who have all helped me to articulate this book in so many ways. I first read Bhaktivedanta Swami's *Bhagavad Gītā As It Is* some 30 or so years ago, and that not only inspired me but influenced my understanding of the *Gītā* ever since. Howard Reznick inspired me to engage with the *Gītā* in a philosophical way, and so did Shlomo Biderman as well as Bhūrijana dāsa. Keith Ward helped me in considering the *Gītā* from a theological point of view, and Klaus Klostermaier helped me articulate these ideas within the context of Hinduism. Francis Clooney S.J. encouraged me to first publish a Hebrew edition, Amram Peter and Alex Cherniak were always there to offer advice and my friends at the Oxford Centre for Hindu Studies, and especially Kiyokazu Okita, engaged in dialogue and offered critical remarks regarding my overall articulation of the *Bhagavad Gītā*'s structure. My students at the University of Haifa were keen to study the *Gītā* according to these lines, and encouraged me by showing how my structure simplified issues considerably and enabled grasping the entire *Gītā* as a unified text. Julius Lipner not only invited me to finalize the manuscript as a Visiting Fellow at the University of Cambridge, but has inspired me as an exemplary *Bhagavad Gītā* scholar. Sarah Lloyd and Lianne Sherlock have taken the book through the editorial and production process. Gail Welsh and Betty Rosen helped with the English editing, and Matthew Kessell accepted the role of the Sanskrit editor. A special thank you goes to my father Emanuel who tirelessly contributed to the editing of this edition, and warm thanks go to my wife, Michal, who, as always, lovingly supported me and my work continuously. At last, deep thanks to my three daughters, Inbal Jāhnavī, Nili Nīla Mādhava devī and Kamah Kamalinī, who bore the burden of this work and encouraged me in various loving ways; it is to them that this book is dedicated.

General Introduction

The *Bhagavad Gītā* is a literary and theological treatise and a foremost world classic; it has occupied both an authoritative and popular position within Hinduism for the last 1,000 years or so. Due to its major influence, it is sometimes called 'The Hindu Bible' or even 'The Indian Bible'; moreover, innumerable people worldwide are able to quote it – whether in their mother language or in the original Sanskrit – as an expression of their faith or worldview. The treatise itself appears as part of the *Mahābhārata*,[1] the great Indian epos, and comprises a dialogue conducted between two of its heroes – the commander-in-chief Arjuna and his cousin, charioteer and friend, Kṛṣṇa. Although the dialogue is rather short and does not exceed 700 verses, it is engaged with subject matters of the highest theological and philosophical order; as such, it concerns everyone who faces human existence, namely each and every human being. The epical circumstances are rather dramatic; due to a long family strife, all the world's armies gather at the battlefield of *Kurukṣetra*, some supporting one family branch, the *Pāṇḍavas* or the sons of Pāṇḍu, while the others supporting the Kauravas, or the sons of Dhṛtarāṣṭra. Arjuna foresees the massacre about to take place, and is reluctant to direct his weapons towards his family members, friends and teachers; as such he desires to relinquish the war altogether and avoid fighting in these terrible circumstances. Out of his deep distress, Arjuna turns to his friend Kṛṣṇa, and asks for directions which may rescue him from this severe crisis. Answering Arjuna, Kṛṣṇa speaks the *Bhagavad Gītā*, which may be possibly translated somewhat roughly as the 'Song of God', or perhaps more precisely as the 'Supreme Person's Sacred Poetical Treatise'. It is likely that the *Bhagavad Gītā* was composed around the fourth to the second centuries BCE, and as such belongs roughly to the same period as that of the great Greek philosophers, Plato and Aristotle. From the religious point of view, the *Bhagavad Gītā* is a *Vaiṣṇava* text, as it considers Viṣṇu or Kṛṣṇa to be the Supreme Lord, whereas from the philosophical point of view, the *Bhagavad Gītā* comprises one of the triple foundations of the *Vedānta* tradition,[2] along with the *Brahmasūtras* and the *Upaniṣads*. From the cultural and social point of view, the *Bhagavad Gītā* represents orthodox and mainstream Hinduism, in that it accepts the authority of the *Veda*, and the social-religious order of four social groups called *Varṇāśrama*, which is at the heart of *dharma*.

---

1 Chapters 23–40 of the *Bhīṣmaparvan*.

2 *Prasthāna trayī*.

Dharma as Comprising and Defining Human Society

The term *dharma* is central to Indian thought, and may be translated as religion, duty, morality, justice, law and order. *Dharma* is not only external to the human being, rather it is perceived as comprising the essence or nature of everything. As such, it aspires to place everything – not only the human being but the whole of phenomena, in its proper place. Thus, for example, the *dharma* of the teacher is to teach, and the *dharma* of the sun is to shine. *Dharma* aspires to establish human society on a solid moral foundation and, as such, it defines the human being through two parameters which are the personal and professional statuses. The personal status is defined through one's relation to family life, and it is comprised by dividing human life into four stages. As such, one spends his childhood and youth as a celibate student, a *brahmacārī*, practicing austerity and discipline while living devoid of possessions under the direction of the *guru*. Along with the character-building one undergoes, he studies the spiritual traditions and develops awareness of the highest truth named *Brahman*. Having concluded his training period, he enters the stage of married life called *gṛhastha*, and fulfils the four aims of life; he follows *dharma* and contributes to the maintenance of the social order, he accumulates wealth, satisfies his desires, and eventually turns his attention towards *mokṣa*, the ideal of liberation from the cycle of birth and death. Once his children have grown up, he gradually returns to the more renounced mode of life practiced during youth, and enters into the *vānaprastha* stage along with his wife. Gradually, the couple becomes detached from family, social, economic and political matters, and turns their attention towards more spiritual matters. At the last stage of one's life, one becomes a *sannyāsī*, and renounces the world altogether, both internally and externally. In this stage he meets death, and being enlightened and detached, he is able to get freed from the vicious cycle of rebirth.

The second parameter defining the human being is the professional one; as such, *dharma* defines four occupational groups which cover the entire range of occupations, supporting a proper human society. The first group is that of the brahmins, who, according to the ancient *Vedic* metaphor, comprise the head of the social body. This is the intellectual class, comprised of teachers, priests, philosophers and intellectuals, and they are characterized by qualities such as tranquility, self-restraint, austerity, purity, tolerance, honesty, knowledge, wisdom and religious piety. They guide and advise human society and they do this from a distant position, without assuming political or governmental authority. The second group is that of the *kṣatriyas*, who, according to the *Vedic* metaphor, comprise the arms of the social body. This is the ruling class comprised of kings, nobles, generals and administrators, and they are characterized by heroism, ardor, determination, expertise, fighting spirit, generosity and leadership. The third group is that of the *vaiśyas* or the agriculture and mercantile class; they comprise the hips of the social body and support society through establishing a firm economic foundation based upon agriculture and trade. The fourth group, the *śūdras*, comprise the legs or feet of the social body, and this is the working and serving class, which includes artisans and craftsmen. The system itself is considered to be of a divine origin, and moreover, not be artificially enforced upon human society, rather to be springing from natural categories and human nature. As such, Kṛṣṇa says that 'the four social classes were created by me according to the divisions of the *guṇas*[3] and modes of work'.[4] *Dharma* is upheld through adhering to one's duties, and the *Bhagavad Gītā* supports this principle, by advising or requesting each and every one to adhere to his or her duty. As such, it says: 'Better to be deficient in following one's own *dharmic* duty, than to perform another's duty well; even death while performing one's own duty is better, for following another's duty invites danger'.[5] Apparently, this idea of the four *varṇas* or classes is philosophical rather than empirical.[6]

Mokṣa – the Call for Relinquishing the World of Birth and Death Altogether

The ideal moral world which is aimed at by *dharma* is doomed to confront human reality which is naturally less ideal, as human existence which is full of weaknesses and faults is somewhat different than the ideal *dharmic* world which is somewhat utopian. This gap occupies a major part of the *Mahābhārata*, where, on the one hand, a description of persons who were able to adhere to *dharma* despite various obstacles is given, and on the other hand, various human weaknesses which prevent one from adherence to duty are delineated. This more pessimistic view of the world leads to the understanding that human existence is ultimately doomed to suffering, and that the only real solution to this problem is the relinquishment of the world altogether. This call, characterizing the *Upaniṣadic* literature and the *Vedāntin* tradition, calls upon the human being to undergo a process of self-correction or self-realization, and altogether relinquish the vicious cycle of birth and death called *saṁsāra*. Accordingly, this world, which is temporary and transient, is never to be considered one's highest goal, as it is of lesser value than the principle or person from whom the world has emanated. As such, the *Bhagavad Gītā* states: 'Having come to me, these great souls do not again undergo rebirth into that transient abode of misery, as they have attained the highest perfection. All the worlds, up to Brahmā's world, are subject to repeated births, but having once reached me, there is no further rebirth.'[7] This well exemplifies the *Upaniṣadic* idea according to which one should relinquish this world in favour of a higher, imperishable perfect and eternal state, which is the state of liberation or *mokṣa*.

---

[3] Quality, constituent; for a more elaborate explanation of the term see p. 9.

[4] *BG* 4.13.

[5] *BG* 3.35.

[6] As a philosophical treatise, the *Bhagavad Gītā* furthers the idea of four classes or *varṇas*, whereas the present-day Indian empirical reality, which may be historically derived from the *Vedic* ideal of four classes, is characterized by *jātis* or hundreds of social subdivisions.

[7] *BG* 8.15–16.

The Tension between *Dharma* and *Mokṣa*

Whereas *dharma* aspires for the moral upliftment of the world and the establishment of a proper and prosperous human society, the *Upaniṣadic* ideal is entirely different and even contradictory, as it calls for a total relinquishment of this world, along with the helpless transmigration from one body to another which characterizes it. Moreover, the *Upaniṣadic* tradition calls one to transcend *dharma*, to go beyond morality and the quest for social order, in favour of a state of introspection and a constant thrust towards self-realization and liberation from the cycle of birth and death. The *Bhagavad Gītā* states that 'for one who is delighted in the self alone, and is thus self satisfied and self content indeed, for him – no *dharmic* duty exists'.[8] It seems that the *Upaniṣadic* tradition is not that concerned with morality and social order, rather it is mainly concerned with the relinquishment of this world and with self-realization. The idea that one who is established in the path of liberation is free from *dharmic* and moral obligations is rather extreme and no doubt exemplifies the deep gap between these two systems of thought.

The *dharma* and *Upaniṣadic* traditions are opposed to each other in yet another cardinal question, and that is the question of action versus knowledge. The *dharma* tradition carries a notable performative flavour, which may have its origins traced back to the ancient *Vedic Mīmāṁsā* school, whereas the *Upaniṣadic* tradition is different in that it emphasizes knowledge over action. *Dharma* aspires to organize the world through action; the brahmin teaches and sacrifices, the *kṣatriya* rules and protects, the *vaiśya* farms and trades and the *śūdra* works manually. The *Upaniṣadic* tradition aspires to reach the understanding or knowing of the essence of all things, which is ultimately spiritual. Moreover, it encourages the renunciation of action and of worldly involvement, in favour of the attainment of real knowledge and enlightenment. The question is raised by Arjuna, and he asks for a clear direction which is the path to be followed; the path of action and adherence to duty, or the path of renunciation of duty in favour of enlightenment. He asks: 'O Janārdana, if you consider enlightenment to be better than action, why then do you enjoin me to perform this terrible act? Your equivocal like words confuse my mind; I beg you, make me certain of one thing, by which I may attain the best.'[9]

The *Bhagavad Gītā* occupies a unique place in the history of Indian literature and thought in that it reconciles this deep tension and gap. On the one hand the *Bhagavad Gītā* adheres to *dharma* by enjoining the following of one's duty in accordance with the *varṇāśrama* system, thereby supporting the moral and social order. At the same time, it supports the *Upaniṣadic* ideal of renouncing the world altogether in favour of self-realization and the attainment of liberation, but propounds the unique and groundbreaking idea of an internal relinquishment, rather than an external one. In other words, as opposed to an external relinquishment, where ones leaves home and social responsibility in favour of becoming a

8 *BG* 3.17.

9 *BG* 3.1–2.

wandering mendicant or a forest-dweller, the *Bhagavad Gītā* furthers an internal relinquishment, by which one adheres to *dharma*, but makes an internal progress along the path of renunciation, by gradually learning to renounce the fruits of action, and then devote them to the supreme. This interesting reconciliation of the two otherwise contradictory ideals, offers a system which intertwines social responsibility and action in the world, with a deep sense of spirituality and relinquishment of worldly attachments. A famous verse propounding this internal renunciation says: 'Your sole entitlement is to perform *dharmic* activity, not ever to possess its fruits; never shall the fruit of an action motivate your deed, and never cleave to inaction.'[10]

The *Bhagavad Gītā*'s Unifying Structure

The *Bhagavad Gītā* is no doubt a unique literary creation, but at the same time deciphering its meaning and philosophy is not easy or simple. Klaus Klostermaier refers to the challenge facing the reader in understanding the *Bhagavad Gītā*:

> Whoever reads it for the first time will be struck by its beauty and depth; countless Hindus know it by heart and quote it in many occasions as an expression of their faith and their insights. All over India, and also in many places in the Western hemisphere, *Gītā* lectures attract large numbers of people. Many are convinced that the *Bhagavad Gītā* is the key book for the respiritualization of humankind in our age. A careful study of the *Gītā*, however, will very soon reveal the need for a key to this key book. Simple as the tale may seem and popular as the work has become, it is by no means an easy book and some of the greatest Indianists have grappled with the historical and philosophical problems it presents.[11]

These words no doubt touch upon one of the main challenges in understanding this treatise; can it be tied together by a relatively simple and unifying theme or structure? I believe that this is possible, and in order to understand the *Bhagavad Gītā*'s structure and main theme, I offer the metaphor of a three-storey house. This house not only has three floors, storeys or tiers, but has a staircase or ladder, leading the residents from the first floor to the second, and from the second to the third. The lower floor represents human life in this world, the second floor is an intermediate floor, whereby one relinquishes worldly life and seeks the state of liberation, and the third floor represents full absorption in the liberated state. The stages of the staircase or the ladder are comprised of various states of action categorized according to their underlying motivation; at the lower stage one's acts are motivated by some utilitarian principle or gain; a stage still higher is when one

---

[10] *BG* 2.47.

[11] Klaus Klostermaier, *A Survey of Hinduism* (2nd edition, Albany, 1994), p. 99.

seeks gain beyond this life in the heavenly world, and a higher stage is the stage of relinquishment of action's fruits, thus acting for the sake of duty or *dharma* alone. A state still higher is the performance of one's *dharmic* duty as a practice of *yoga*, i.e. considering the performance of duty to be the means by which the mind may be subdued. The highest state is the state of performing one's *dharmic* duty while being liberated and entirely immersed in the supreme. In this way, the *Bhagavad Gītā* adheres to both ideals; it supports social responsibility, morality and *dharma*, and at the same time, it endorses the *Upaniṣadic* path of self-realization, which leads one from the depth of material existence all the way up to liberation.[12]

The *Vedic* Sacrifices and the Humanistic View of the 'First Tier'

Vedic ritualistic sacrifices were common in ancient India; some sacrifices were domestic whereas others were public, some were simple whereas others were sophisticated and expensive. Underlying all the various sacrifices was a deep faith in the perfection of the *Veda*, and the conviction that sacrifice is the way for the attainment of prosperity, both in this life and the next. A major purpose or fruit to be achieved by the performance of the *Vedic* sacrifice was the attainment of heaven; it is not entirely clear where exactly heaven is situated; it may be taken geographically, as a particular higher planet, but also as a higher state of existence. It is apparent, however, that heavenly life was considered to be a more pleasurable existential state, and that normally one would aspire to achieve this state in the next life. Heaven's opposite was considered to exist too, and that is hell; whether this refers to a geographical place, apparently located at the bottom of the universe, or whether this refers to a lower state of existence, it is apparent that according to *Vedic* thought, hellish life is a state of suffering and should be avoided. Accordingly, the *Vedas* are considered eternal and perfect, and hence the somewhat problematic position of the *Vedic* sacrifices and rituals; on the one hand, some claim that as the *Vedas* are of a divine origin, it is one's sacred duty to perform *Vedic* sacrifice and attain prosperity, both in this life and the next. Others, who further the path of liberation, agree that the *Vedas* are of a divine origin, but consider the ultimate goal to be the renunciation of worldly pleasures and prosperity in favour of liberation. As such, they consider worldly prosperity as a blessing which should be accepted moderately, but certainly not as the ultimate goal; accordingly, worldly prosperity should be considered as a healthy condition of a society which is gradually progressing towards liberation. Considering the above said, it seems that the *Vedic* worldview represents what we call the 'first storey'; it is optimistic as it aspires for healthy, moral, proper and prosperous human life. In that, it aspires to avoid that which is immoral and unjust and further that which is healthy and righteous. It is humanistic in that it perceives reality

[12] A deeper analysis of the *Bhagavad Gītā*'s structure follows the General Introduction. See p. 17.

in complete and unbroken terms centred around the human being; as such, its worldview is constructed by terms such as the human being, the family, society and, above all, *dharma* which constantly thrives to uplift human society.

The Embodied Soul, the Problem of Transmigration and the *Yogic* View of the 'Second Tier'

The main problem characterizing this world, and even the next or the heavenly world, is the constant repetition of birth and death. The constant change, the inherent instability, the encagement of an otherwise free spiritual soul in a body destined to die, the constant struggle with the senses and their unsatiated desires, all these make the worldly and embodied state undesirable. Moreover, seen from the *Bhagavad Gītā*'s second tier's point of view, even the state of heavenly life, which can be attained through the performance of *Vedic* sacrifices, is flawed by this vicious cycle of birth and death. In other words, having spent prolonged periods of time in the enjoyable heavenly state, one falls down again into the lower worlds and into lower states of existence. This vision naturally leads to an attempt to get free from this embodied state, by taking to the process of self-realization, which includes a different set of categories. Progressing along the path of self-realization, one begins to think of himself or herself in different terms; instead of considering oneself to be a human being, one starts thinking of himself as an eternal spiritual soul, rather different to the gross and subtle coverings, i.e. the body and the mind, which cover and encage him. As such, it is said: 'As childhood, youth and old age befall the soul within this body, so it comes to acquire another body; the wise is not swayed by illusion in this matter.'[13]

This point of view is what we may call a 'second storey' one; from this point of view one sees his own body and mind as external to himself, considers his deep entanglement with matter to be circumstantial, non-essential and an obstacle on the path of liberation, and in this state he tries not only to sever his deep relations with matter and mind, but to gain hold of the spiritual reality of *Brahman*, in either its personal or impersonal form. This worldview or the vision of the soul, i.e. the 'second storey' worldview, does not really aim at constructing a prosperous and moral human society, rather, it furthers the relinquishment of this world altogether. It is not really humanistic, as the term 'human being' does not play a very significant role in it, rather the term 'spiritual soul' seems to construct the individual identities in this view, and as such it may be considered a 'spiritualistic' view. As such, the fundamental individual element is the spiritual soul, covered by various bodies which are not necessarily human; these may be bodies of plants, trees, reptiles, fish, animals, humans or gods, etc. This worldview, which is based upon the vision of spiritual souls encaged in gross and subtle bodies, has an ethical implication, too; as it envisions souls encaged in bodies, it naturally

---

[13] *BG* 2.13.

furthers the release of those embodied souls. As such, it furthers a different set of values than those of the 'first storey'; instead of furthering human prosperity, it propounds equanimity towards both the good and the bad, towards both happiness and distress, towards both prosperity and poverty, and towards both the moral and the immoral. This equanimity serves as a foundation based upon which one can look beyond this world and search after the spiritual reality which is utterly different, and is designated as eternal, conscious and blissful. As such, there are two components of the 'second storey': one the one hand, the attempt to release oneself from the embodied state, and on the other hand, the attempt to establish or yoke oneself within the supreme, absolute and spiritual reality. As these two principles, i.e. attempting to detach oneself from this world and attempting to yoke oneself to a higher state or reality, underlie the various *yoga* systems, this view may also be considered the '*yogic* view'.

Mental Restraint as the Focus of the Various *Yoga* Systems

The various *yoga* systems all aspire to transfer the practitioner from the state of worldly existence, into the enlightened and liberated state. The practice focuses on the mind,[14] which in the unrestrained state binds the soul to embodiment, while in the restrained and transparent state it leads the soul to liberation. The mind unites the physical body, the senses and the soul, and is considered to have an immense capability of leading the soul towards enlightenment. However, being unrestrained, disturbed and obscure due to its close relation with the senses and the various worldly desires aroused by them, it fails to realize its potential. The *yoga* systems, therefore, aspire to restrain and clean the mind, just like one cleans a mirror or a lens for the purpose of seeing clearly. In its obscure state, the mind is disturbed by the working of nature represented by the three *guṇas*, by agitation aroused by attraction, by repulsion aroused by sense objects, by misconceptions of the self and various memories, and by the urge of self-preservation and the fear of death. A clear consciousness may be compared to a clear and peaceful lake, which is transparent and, as such, its bottom may be viewed, while an obscure consciousness may be compared to a stormy lake of muddy water, which is naturally non-transparent and its bottom unseen. The two core principles of the *yoga* system are practice and detachment; while practice aims at the gradual restraint of the turbulent mind, detachment aims at disconnecting the mind from the various sense objects to which it is attached. Chapter 6 is engaged with this topic and advises the practitioner of *yoga*: 'Casting aside all desires arising from worldly intentions, he should subdue completely the combined senses through the mind. Little by little should he bring his mind to rest, while firmly controlling his consciousness; he should fix his mind on the self, contemplating nothing else.

---

[14] Sanskrit: *manas*.

From whatever and wherever the flickering and unsteady mind wanders, it is to be restrained and led back into the control of the self.'[15]

The *yoga* system is not merely theoretical, rather it furthers a psycho-physic practice. The classical text *Yogasūtra*, traditionally attributed to Patañjali,[16] articulates an eight-stage ladder-like structure which, in a sense, serves as an archetype for the *yoga* system; the eight stages commence with practices which may be considered ethical, and culminate with the stage of *samādhi*, a liberated state of enstasy or enlightenment. The first stage is called *yama* or restraint, and it includes the practice of non-violence, adherence to truthfulness, non-stealing, the practice of *brahmacārya* which includes sexual abstinence, and non-accumulation. The second stage is *niyama*, and it is comprised of cleanliness or purity, satisfaction, austerity, self-study and scriptural study, and devotion to the supreme. The third stage, *āsana*, includes an elaborate practice of bodily postures, and this is followed by *prāṇāyāma*, the stage of breath control. Following that one practices *pratyāhāra* or the withdrawal of the senses from their objects, and this is followed by *dhāraṇā* or concentration in which one strives to maintain this sense withdrawal over an extended period of time. The seventh stage is that of *dhyāna* and its essence is meditation on the supreme, while the peak of the system is the eighth stage called *samādhi*, in which the *yogī* enters a state of an introspective enlightenment beyond worldly existence. This state is described in Chapter 6: 'When the consciousness rests peacefully, restrained by practice of *yoga*, then can the self see itself directly, and be thus satisfied within itself. At that time he knows infinite bliss, experienced by an internal consciousness beyond the senses; firmly established, he deviates not from the truth. Having attained this, he holds no other acquisition greater, and thus situated, even grievous misery does not shake him. Let it be known that dissolution of the deep union with misery is called *yoga*, and it should be practiced with whole-hearted determination.'[17]

Human Nature as Comprised of the Three *Guṇas*

The theory underlying the *Yoga* and *Sāṅkhya* schools considers nature to consist of three qualities or strands, called *guṇas*; the three qualities are named *sattva* representing goodness and transparency, *rajas* representing passion and desire, and *tamas* representing ignorance, indolence and darkness. The three *guṇas* comprise human nature, and they bind the soul to mind and matter, or to the subtle and gross bodies. As opposed to the soul which remains steady and unchanging, the *guṇas* constantly interact among themselves, and unite in various combinations; as such, sometimes goodness prevails, sometimes passion and sometimes darkness. As the *guṇas* are so dominant and govern every aspect of life, this world is sometimes

[15] *BG* 6.24–26.

[16] Second to third century CE.

[17] *BG* 6.20–23.

called 'the world of the *guṇas*'. As the three *guṇas* comprise human nature, they are reflected through each and every thought, word or deed. As such, the way one thinks, speaks and acts reflects the combination of the conditioning *guṇas*. This concept offers a unique division of human and even non-human existence which groups together various aspects of life, such as various psychological components, activity and adherence to duty, social grouping, eating habits and cosmological divisions. The *guṇa* of goodness is characterized by knowledge and happiness, and adherence to duty for the sake of duty; it represents the intellectual social group or the brahmins, is associated with fresh vegetarian food and, cosmologically, leads to the higher planets. The *guṇa* of passion is characterized by desire and attachment, and with adherence to duty for the sake of its fruits or for some ulterior gain; when mixed with a larger amount of goodness it represents the ruling class, and when mixed with a somewhat lesser amount of goodness, it represents the mercantile and farming class. It is associated with vegetarian food which agitates the senses, such as spicy or salty food, and cosmologically it leads to the middle planets. The *guṇa* of ignorance is characterized by darkness, indolence and madness and it involves the negligence of duty; it is more dominant among the productive social class, it is associated with non-vegetarian food and intoxicating drinks, and, cosmologically, it leads to the lower planets.

The *guṇas* may also be thought of as universal paths, on which the soul travels during its journey through *saṁsāra*. The path of goodness seems at first to be somewhat pale, but as one adheres to it, one gradually begins to experience happiness, stability and illumination. The path of passion is contrary, in that it seems very attractive and exciting at first, but as one adheres to it, one begins to experience distress and exhaustion. The lowest path, that of darkness, represents the lowest human condition; it is characterized by indolence, foolishness and even madness, and it leads to self-destruction. Despite the possibility of rationalizing these three paths, it may be rather difficult for the embodied to escape the influence or even bondage of the particular *guṇas* binding him or her. For the *Bhagavad Gīta*, the idea of the *guṇas* is fundamental and elaborate discussions on the nature of the *guṇas* take place, especially in Chapters 14, 17 and 18. The *Bhagavad Gītā* suggests a gradual elevation, by which one raises oneself from a lower *guṇa* to a higher one. For this purpose, various characteristics of the *guṇas*' bondage are delineated, and these enable a process of self-examination or self-study. Consequently, one is able to change one's habits for the purpose of raising oneself in this ladder of the *guṇas*. This idea of the *guṇas* is firmly tied with the ladder-like structure of the *Bhagavad Gītā*; as such, being established in the *guṇa* of goodness, one finds oneself adhering to *dharma*. In other words, when one adheres to *dharma* being motivated by some ulterior motives, one is considered to be governed by the two lower *guṇas*, but when one is able to rise to the *guṇa* of goodness, one practices following *dharma* for its own sake, in a disinterested manner, with no desire for its fruits. This is the highest position one may reach within what we call the 'first storey', and hence one continues to progress towards the 'second storey', towards a position 'beyond the *guṇas*'.

Action and Beyond – the Principle of *Karma*

The *Yogic-Upaniṣadic* point of view[18] which underlies the 'second storey' is somewhat complex in its perception of human action. As the soul is considered eternal, as the *guṇas* act and influence the soul beyond this life, similarly the concept of action is taken to have implications beyond the present life, having its roots in previous lives, and its consequences in future lives. In essence, every action is considered to bear not only immediate consequences, but long-term ones as well. As such, one may give charity to the needy and, as a result, be born in one's next life to a rich family, consequently living an opulent life. Alternatively, one may commit some evil and as a result be born in a poor family and consequently live in difficult conditions. This may also reinforce the vision of the *guṇas* as universal paths; a person influenced by the *guṇa* of goodness gives charity, and this elevates him in his next life to a pious environment where he is well educated and, as such, continues to do good for others and be subsequently further elevated. Alternatively, a person influenced by the lower *guṇas* causes distress to others, and is consequently born in lower conditions or bodies, where a bad nature is enforced upon him and drags him further down the existential root. Although no doubt this concept may suggest the loss of free will and a somewhat fatalistic worldview, the *Bhagavad Gītā* firmly propounds the idea of free will, and underlying the entire conversation is the understanding that Arjuna can choose his own way or path. In other words, this suggests that despite the seeming fatalism sentenced by the *guṇas*, one still has a fair amount of free will, and is able to change one's life course and existence.

Chapter 4 deals extensively with the subject matter of action and states: 'What is action? What is inaction? Even the wise are confused in this matter. Now I shall explain to you this subject matter of action; having known this you shall be free from evil. One must know what action (*karma*) is, one must know what improper action (*vikarma*) is, and one must know what inaction (*akarma*) is, as profound indeed is the course of action.'[19] Proper action is performed in accordance with one's duty or *dharma* and bears good results, whereas improper action is contrary to one's *dharmic* duties and this bears distressing results. Seen from this point of view, both good and bad acts ultimately bind one to continuous existence, as one will have to be born again in order to enjoy or suffer the results or the fruits of his or her actions. Alternatively, one is encouraged to perform a 'clean' or 'pure' action, which is considered to be inaction: the reason is that when this is done in the appropriate way, i.e. without regards to the fruits, accompanied by knowledge

---

18 Apparently the *Upaniṣads* contain also humanistic or *pravṛttic* sections furthering the ideal of *dharma*, and similarly, the *Yoga* traditions too contain ideals furthering humanistic ethics such as the stages of *yama* and *niyama*. Still, overall these traditions emphasize and further an attitude of renunciation or *nivṛtti*, as opposed, say, to traditions such as the *mīmāṁsā*, and as such they could be associated with the concept of the 'second tier'.

19 *BG* 4.16–17.

and as an offering to the supreme, it does not bear consequential fruits in future lives, rather it leads to liberation. As such, it doesn't have the normal binding characteristics of action; this is the highest mode of action proposed at the end of the *Bhagavad Gītā*, in a statement which is sometimes considered to be the text's culmination and peak: 'Abandon all sorts of *dharmas* and take refuge in me alone, and I shall release you from all evils; do not fear.'[20] This raises a question in regards to the relinquishment of duty, or the external abstention from action; it seems that this is taken as a sort of improper action, and as such is liable to bear a bad result. The *Bhagavad Gītā* emphasizes the path of *karma yoga*, which is a *yoga* of action; accordingly, one undergoes the same *yogic* transformation through the performance of action or, more specifically, action according to *dharma*. As such, one examines one's own mode of action, and constantly endeavors to sublimate it; in this way, by adhering to one's duty, by constantly sublimating it and by refining one's inner motivations, one attains enlightenment through action. Arjuna is presented with various motivations for performing his duty and fighting; he may fight out of some utilitarian purposes, he may fight for the sake of duty, his fighting may be taken as a practice of *yoga*, and he may fight out of devotion to the supreme.

The *Bhagavad Gītā*'s Educational Doctrine

Having surveyed the two armies about to fight, Arjuna becomes despondent in his attempt to resolve the seemingly impossible moral dilemma facing him. At that time, he turns to Kṛṣṇa, his friend and charioteer, in a new way; he approaches Kṛṣṇa as a student approaches his *guru*, teacher or master, and declares: 'I am now your disciple and I fall at your feet; please instruct me!'[21] The *guru* teaches his student through personal tutorship, while the student not only learns from the *guru* theoretical knowledge, but also serves his *guru* and aspires to please him. Chapter 4 refers to the *guru*–disciple relationship by saying: 'Know this by falling at the feet of the master, asking him questions and offering him service; in so doing, men of wisdom and vision of the truth will impart knowledge unto you.'[22] This no doubt seems to be a very personal mode of knowledge transmission and it entails character-building and a transfer of values. The structure of the *Bhagavad Gītā* is composed not only of three tiers of reality, rather its other major component is a transformational ladder; the training process offered by the *guru* aspires to further a moral and spiritual transformation, and a gradual elevation along this ladder of values. The *Bhagavad Gītā* begins with the lowest stage of the ladder, represented by Arjuna's lamentation which appears in Chapter 1, it follows a gradual ascendance throughout the entire text, and this ascendance reaches its peak at the end of the last chapter, where Arjuna surrenders himself entirely to Kṛṣṇa.

---

20 *BG* 18.66.

21 *BG* 2.7.

22 *BG* 4.34.

The question may be raised, what is considered to represent proper knowledge according to the *Bhagavad Gītā*, or what is it that the *guru* teaches? Also, are the various components of knowledge organized according to the three stories, too? Chapter 16 offers a list of the divine qualities, and opposes this with the demonic ones:

> Fearlessness, purification of one's whole being, firmness in spiritual knowledge, generosity, self control and sacrifice, studying the *Veda*, austerity, righteousness, nonviolence, truthfulness, absence of anger, renunciation, tranquillity, avoiding vilification, compassion for all beings, absence of greed, gentleness, modesty, reliability, vigour, tolerance, fortitude, purity, absence of envy and pride – these are the qualities of one born to divine destiny, O Bhārata. Hypocrisy, arrogance, conceit, anger, harshness and ignorance – these are the qualities of one who is born to a demonic destiny.[23]

From analysing this list, it seems that these represent what we may call 'first-storey educational ideals'. In other words, these are ideal qualities to be pursued while living in accordance with *dharma*, and their counterparts, the demonic qualities, are to be avoided. Chapter 13 offers a somewhat similar list of qualities, which represent knowledge:

> Absence of pride and arrogance, nonviolence, forbearance, honesty, attendance upon the *guru*, purity, firmness, self control, lack of attraction to sense objects, absence of ego-notion, visioning the distress and evil of birth, death, old age and disease, detachment, aloofness from sons, wife, home and the like, constant equanimity toward desired and undesired events, single-minded devotion to me supported by *yoga*, preferring of solitary places and avoiding the crowds, constant contemplation of knowledge of the self, envisioning the purpose of knowledge concerned with the truth – all these are declared knowledge, whereas all else is ignorance.[24]

This list seems to be aiming at a somewhat higher position along the ladder, and may be more compatible with the second and *yogic* storey. It is more introspective, emphasizes *yoga*, detachment, absence of ego and the vision of equality. Although it is not as explicit as these two lists, one may find the following verse to supply values which may be considered third-storey ideal qualities:

> Those whose consciousness is absorbed in me, for whom I am everything, enlighten one another about me, constantly speaking of me; thus absorbed, they are delighted and content.[25]

---

[23] *BG* 16.1–4.

[24] *BG* 13.7–11.

[25] *BG* 10.9.

This is a description of devotees immersed in the supreme; they are entirely absorbed in the supreme, they have no other object of interest, and they not only enlighten each other about the supreme, but take great pleasure in doing so. It may well be that implicit in this statement is the idea that this stage of being deeply immersed in the supreme represents not only the highest devotion, but also the highest degree of knowledge.

Bhakti

Bhakti, or devotion, is one of the *Bhagavad Gītā*'s major components; it represents a loving attitude towards the supreme who is generally thought of in the context of *bhakti* in personal terms. Looking deeper into the emotional state characterizing *bhakti*, one may discern love, devotion, a desire to please the Supreme Person, a sense of dependence upon him, a desire to glorify him and share this glorification with other devoted persons or *bhaktas*, a desire to serve the Supreme Lord through one's profession, a sense of loyalty to him, a desire to worship him and a desire to please him by offering various gifts such as flowers or fruits. Kṛṣṇa, who according to the *Bhagavad Gītā* is the Supreme Lord in Person, and who is the object of devotion, is not indifferent to his devotee, rather is very affectionate and protective towards him or her. As opposed to the general masculine voice dominating the *Bhagavad Gītā*, when it comes to devotion, the text specifically refers to female devotees, in a declaration which could be taken as groundbreaking for its time: 'Those who take refuge in me, be they of lowly origin, women, merchants and even servants; even they may attain the highest destination.'[26]

Looking into the structure of the *Bhagavad Gītā*, it becomes evident that *bhakti* serves as a major, or maybe even *the* major, elevating force, which 'pulls', so to speak, or raises one in his transformational journey towards self-transcendence. Although there are other motivations for elevation along the transformational ladder such as the desire to attain true knowledge, the desire to become free from the implications of *karma*, and the desire for a *yogic* perfection, still, *bhakti* is perhaps the central source of inspiration for one to leave this world altogether. The idea of *bhakti* first appears explicitly towards the end of Chapter 3, where Kṛṣṇa urges Arjuna to fight in the mood of surrender unto him: 'Surrendering all your activities unto me with mind fixed on the highest self, without desire and avoiding possessiveness, cast lethargy aside and fight!'[27] Arjuna's reaction follows soon after, and at the beginning of Chapter 4 he asks about Kṛṣṇa's identity,[28] to which Kṛṣṇa answers that he is the Lord of all beings descending to uphold *dharma*. Following that, Kṛṣṇa encourages Arjuna in numerous places throughout the *Bhagavad Gītā*, to take refuge in him in a devotional mood. In general, Kṛṣṇa

---

[26] *BG* 9.32.

[27] *BG* 3.30.

[28] *BG* 4.4.

urges Arjuna to become his devotee in three basic ways or rather stages, which are compatible with the three tiers of the text. On the first tier, Kṛṣṇa encourages Arjuna to adhere to his work and duty according to *dharma*, and offer this work and its results unto him. An example for this kind of devotion is found at the end of Chapter 9: 'Whatever you do, whatever you eat, whatever you offer in sacrifice, whatever you give away and whatever austerity you may practice, O Kaunteya, do it as an offering unto me.'[29] Underlying this statement is the understanding that Arjuna is thinking in terms of 'the world of *dharma*'; as such, he is encouraged to maintain his sense of human individuality, and to offer Kṛṣṇa the fruits of his work. A higher state of *bhakti* is that of *yogic* devotion exemplified by Kṛṣṇa's conclusion of Chapter 4: 'Therefore, O Bharata, you should cut the doubt residing in your heart which springs from nothing but ignorance, with your own sword of knowledge, resort to *yoga* and rise up to battle!'[30] This represents a 'second storey' position, where Arjuna is attempting to rise above his own worldly attachments, represented by the doubts residing in his heart, and obstructing him from hearing Kṛṣṇa clearly and following his instructions. Kṛṣṇa urges him to cut his doubts, which represent ignorance, with the sword of knowledge, and doing so by resorting to *yoga*. A verse which seems to carry a similar import, although with a slightly more personal emphasis, may be found in Chapter 8: 'Therefore, at all times remember me and fight; with your mind and intelligence absorbed in me, you will come to me without doubt.'[31] This verse also relates the external fighting to the internal one; the fighting here is considered to be a kind of a *yoga* practice, involving sense restraint, mental control and an inner meditation upon Kṛṣṇa. As such, it well exemplifies the two main components of the 'second storey' or the world of *yoga*; one the one hand, attempting to cut the bonds which hold one in embodied existence, and on the other hand, an attempt to connect or yoke oneself to the higher, supreme and spiritual reality, here represented by Kṛṣṇa himself. The 'third storey' *bhakti* may be exemplified by two of the *Bhagavad Gītā*'s concluding verses: 'Always think of me, become my devotee, worship me and pay your homage to me, and thus you shall undoubtedly come to me; I promise you this as you are dear to me. Abandon all *dharmas* and take refuge in me alone, and I shall release you from all evils; do not fear.'[32] These two verses represent a higher and more peaceful state of devotion to Kṛṣṇa; this is the state beyond both *dharma* and the internal *yogic* struggle, a state of intense but peaceful absorption in the mood of devotion, in which one always thinks of Kṛṣṇa in loving devotion, and is very dear to Kṛṣṇa. A more structured and condensed description of a descending 'ladder of devotion' appears in Chapter 12:

[29] *BG* 9.27.

[30] *BG* 4.42.

[31] *BG* 8.7.

[32] *BG* 18.65–66.

> Fix your mind on me alone, and absorb your consciousness in me; thus you shall surely abide in me. If you cannot fix your consciousness steadily upon me, then aspire to reach me through repeated *yoga* practice, O Dhanañjaya. If you are incapable even of that, embrace the path of action, for which I am the highest goal, since by acting for me you shall attain perfection. But if you are even unable to follow this path of refuge in me through acts devoted to me, then give up the fruits of all your actions, thus restraining yourself. Knowledge is superior to practice, meditation is superior to knowledge, and relinquishing the fruits of actions is higher than meditation, as tranquillity soon follows such relinquishment.[33]

The ladder begins with a complete absorption of one's consciousness in Kṛṣṇa which is a 'third tier' position. The next and lower stage is a direct *yoga* practice, and the next stage is working for Kṛṣṇa and offering him the fruits of labour; both of these stages represent a 'second tier' position. Lower than that is the 'first tier' position of relinquishing the fruits of labour; following that come meditation, knowledge and practice.

The Vision of the Supreme

The *Bhagavad Gītā* reaches its theological climax in Chapters 7 and 9, where the vision of the 'third storey' is articulated. Having lead Arjuna from the first storey to the second, and then to the third, Kṛṣṇa at last relinquishes the various logical arguments meant to convince Arjuna to rise higher and higher along the ladder of self-transcendence, and turns to a description of the spiritual reality. Kṛṣṇa speaks of his complex relationships with the spiritual souls and the world, moving between transcendence and immanence; as such, he describes two natures, the lower and the higher: 'Earth, water, fire, air, ether, mind, intellect and ego – these eight comprise my separated lower nature; but you should know that beside this lower nature, O mighty-armed one, there is another higher nature of mine, comprised of spirit souls, by which this world is sustained.'[34] Both of these natures are Kṛṣṇa's natures, but the first which is comprised of matter and mind is lower and separated, whereas the second which is comprised of spiritual souls is higher and apparently connected or deeply related to Kṛṣṇa, who himself supports the entire creation, as everything rests upon him just like pearls which are strung on a thread.[35] The relationships between the Supreme Person and the creation are complex and much has been said and written in this regards by the later great *Vedāntin* commentators, who articulated systematic theologies engaged with the dualism and the non-dualism of the world. The text continues to endow a vision:

33 *BG* 12.8–12.

34 *BG* 7.4–5.

35 *BG* 7.7.

> I pervade the entire world in my unmanifest form; all beings rest in me, but I do not rest in them, and yet all beings do not rest in me. See my mystic splendour! I sustain beings but rely not on them; my very self is the cause of their being. 6 As the great wind that goes everywhere is eternally contained within space, know that similarly all beings are contained in me.[36]

This description is free from argumentative language, and it may be difficult to articulate it within common theological categories such as transcendence, immanence or pantheism. These statements do not seem to adhere to simple logic; as such, all beings rest in Kṛṣṇa, but at the same time all beings do not rest in him. The reason is that this description comprises a *darśana* or vision. This vision is not open to all, rather one must become a surrendered devotee of Kṛṣṇa in order to overcome his deluding power and maintain such a vision: 'Divine indeed and difficult to penetrate is my deluding power, consisting of the three *guṇas*; but those who have surrendered unto me alone, they can transcend it.'[37] As such, one must overcome desires and become a surrendered devotee of Kṛṣṇa in order to absorb and maintain such a vision. Chapter 9 concludes with a statement which seems to represent the epitome of the entire *Bhagavad Gītā*, and this is a call for pure devotion: 'Always think of me and become my devotee, worship me and pay homage unto me; thus yoked to me and intent on me as your highest goal, you shall come to me.'[38]

Looking into the Structure of the *Bhagavad Gītā*

So far we have presented the *Bhagavad Gītā*'s structure in a somewhat simplistic manner; we may now examine it more carefully. The *Bhagavad Gītā* is a rich treatise containing numerous ideas fundamental to Hinduism; however, are these ideas consistent and coherent? Seen from a theological-philosophical perspective, the *Bhagavad Gītā* possesses a coherent and consistent theme, which could be followed from the beginning of the treatise to its end. This section aims at looking deeper into the *Bhagavad Gītā*'s structure which is founded on a three-tier concept of reality, and intertwined with a transformational ethical ladder. The idea of hierarchical reality suggests that reality is not unified, rather that it contains differing tiers or levels; there is a higher reality as well as a lower reality, and one must distinguish between the two. Moreover, each tier has its own unique language, terms and underlying assumptions. The ethical ladder is composed of various stages, and these enable one to rise from the lower tier of reality, to the intermediate tier and then to the higher one. Each of the ladder's stages is defined by its underlying motivation; the more one undergoes transformation through the

[36] *BG* 9.4–6.

[37] *BG* 7.14.

[38] *BG* 9.34.

sublimation of one's motives for action, the more one transcends this ethical ladder. The ethical ladder is rooted at the lower stage of reality which represents worldly life, and as one gradually rises up the ladder, one makes progress towards the state of *mokṣa*.[39] This structure highlights the *Bhagavad Gītā*'s *jñāna* and *karma* aspects; the *jñāna* aspect is represented by the three-tier metaphysical concept, whereas the *karma* aspect is represented by the ladder of action's various grades. The three metaphysical tiers and the ladder of ethical stages are complementary; the division of reality into these three tiers highlights one's present condition in the lower tier, and one's goal which is the higher tier, whereas the ladder of action provides the practical means of gradually overcoming this gap step by step, by a process of self-transformation.

Hierarchical Reality in the *Bhagavad Gītā*

The *Bhagavad Gītā* is one of the triple foundations of *Vedānta*, and as such shares qualities characterizing a *Vedāntin* text, such as hierarchical grades of reality. In general, one can find two principal metaphysical positions in Indian philosophy; the realistic or direct position and the hierarchical position. The direct-realistic position assumes that reality is unified, that is, it does not contain divisions or layers; as such it is subject to direct human recognition and should not be submitted to different interpretations. The hierarchical position assumes that reality is not unified, rather contains differing levels or tiers. There is a higher or superior reality, and a lower or inferior reality, and one must distinguish between absolute and relative reality.[40] The two-levelled reality concept, the first empirical and conventional and the second absolute, the first changing and finite, and the second permanent and infinite, may be treated by applying the terminology '*dharma*' and '*mokṣa*'; the level of *dharma* is representative of the human or worldly condition, while the level of *mokṣa* is representative of the real or absolute condition.

Mentioning *dharma*, its opposite term, *adharma*, ought to be referred to as well. Ordinarily, *dharma* and *adharma* are considered opposite terms; however, seen from the point of view of *mokṣa*, both *dharma* and *adharma* are in an entirely different category. According to our terminology, both *dharma* and *adharma* represent the finite level, whereas *mokṣa* represents the infinite level. Simplifying terms, the embodied state representing both *dharma* and *adharma* is the world of *saṁsāra*, whereas the liberated state is of an entirely different nature called *mokṣa*. These two kinds of dichotomies – between *dharma* and *adharma*, and between *dharma* and *mokṣa*, can be understood through a somewhat graphic description: the dichotomy between *dharma* and *adharma* may be taken to be horizontal, as both existing within the same realm, whereas the dichotomy between both *dharma*

---

[39] The idea of the ladder is traditional. See; 'The Yoga Ladder' in: Bhūrijana Dāsa, *Surrender Unto Me* (New Delhi, 1997), pp. 59–68.

[40] Shlomo Biderman, *Indian Philosophy – The Foundations* (Tel Aviv, 1980), p. 61.

and *adharma* and between *mokṣa*, may be taken to be vertical. This is so as both *dharma* and *adharma* are situated in the worldly or finite level, whereas *mokṣa* is situated in a completely different and higher level which is infinite and absolute. Besides the two tiers underlying the *Bhagavad Gītā* – which could be considered the finite and the infinite, or alternatively, *dharma* and *mokṣa* – there is a third tier, serving as an intermediate one connecting the two tiers, which would otherwise be unrelated to each other due to an insurmountable gap separating the two. The first tier represents *dharma*, and furthers proper human life. The second tier represents *yoga*, and furthers attempts to escape the viscous state of *saṁsāra* while gradually seeking hold of the state of *mokṣa*, and the third tier represents the state of *mokṣa* itself.

A question may arise, 'How can these tiers be studied or distinguished?' I suggest that in order to distinguish the tiers from each other, their underlying assumptions in terms of values and being may be examined.[41] Thus in the first tier, that of *dharma*, the general rule in terms of value is to prosper; as such, worldly happiness and prosperity are desired and are good. In terms of being, the individual is defined in this tier as a human being or any other living being such as an animal, plant or other. In the second tier, the value of worldly prosperity is rejected in favour of non-attachment to the world and indifference to both worldly happiness and worldly distress, along with yoking oneself to a higher reality, that of *mokṣa*. In terms of being, the individual person does not consider himself any longer a human (or other) being but as an eternal spiritual soul bound by the laws of *saṁsāra*. Thus the individual's subjective identity is not any more a human being, rather that of an eternal spiritual soul. In the third tier the ideal value is the experience of *brahmananda* or the bliss of *Brahman*; this realization takes place within the wider context of the Supreme Person who is the foundation underlying the immortal and imperishable *Brahman*. Thus, the indifference and non-attachment of the second tier are replaced by deep attachment to the Supreme Person, and deep love expressed by loving feelings towards him. As far as being is concerned, the spiritual soul of the second tier becomes not only pure existence and one with *Brahman*, but assumes the identity of a pure servant and a lover of the Supreme Person.

The three tiers represent internal mental states or attitudes. Thus, one who sees the world from the point of view of the first tier is convinced that he or she is a human being, and that his or her aim is to prosper. Similarly, one who sees the world from the point of view of the second tier is convinced that he is an embodied spiritual self, and that his aim is to get released from that condition. One who resides in the third tier may realize his oneness with *Brahman*, sees the supreme in person everywhere and aspires to serve and love him. I suggest the usage of a three-storey house as a metaphor, with each tier representing a storey or floor, and the ethical ladder serving as a staircase. Each storey or tier contains unlimited existential opportunities and paths; moreover, the residents of each floor have

---

[41] Corresponding to the categories of ethics and ontology.

their own language, terms and underlying assumptions which are different from those of the residents of the other storeys. In a sense, the *Bhagavad Gītā* speaks in three different languages and constantly moves between the three tiers. Once recognizing the storey or tier from which the text is speaking, that section becomes intelligible and consistent with the rest of the treatise. On a more practical level, once recognizing one's ethical stage, it becomes apparent what the next stage of progress is. These distinctions may appear to be somewhat sharp whereas in the text itself there are connecting links between the storeys or tiers. However, this could possibly be compared to the study of grammar, where tables of roots and stems are articulated and discussed; although these linguistic forms are merely theoretical or structural, and do not appear in actual spoken language, they actually underlie it. Similarly the distinction between the tiers underlies the text although in the text itself these distinctions may not always be easy to inspect.

These ideas may be better demonstrated by a textual reference. As such, the following example demonstrates how the text shifts from the first tier to the second; when Arjuna argues against fighting the war, he does so from the position of the first tier:

> When *adharma* overpowers the family its ladies become corrupt, O Kṛṣṇa, and when the women become corrupt there is miscegenation of classes. Surely miscegenation among classes leads both the clan's destroyers and the family itself to hell. The family ancestors fall too, deprived of their due offerings of sanctified food and water. As such, the evil deeds of the destroyers which lead to miscegenation among classes, wipe out eternal caste and family *dharma*. O Janārdana, we have heard that hell awaits those whose family *dharma* has been obliterated. Alas, resolved are we on committing a great evil, if we intend to kill our own people out of greed for royal pleasure. Better had I been killed on the battlefield, unarmed and unresisting, by Dhṛtarāṣṭra's sons with weapons in their hands.[42]

This passage may now be examined according to the two parameters previously mentioned – values and being. As far as values are concerned, it is clear that underlying Arjuna's speech is a desire for worldly prosperity; he believes that prosperity is good and objects to the war, which would cause the decline of *dharma*, the rise of *adharma* and the infliction of suffering upon all involved and beyond. As far as being is concerned, Arjuna thinks of himself and the others as human beings. In answering Arjuna, Kṛṣṇa doesn't address his concerns directly, but raises the conversation to the second tier and says:

> O Dhṛtarāṣṭra, between both armies, Hṛsīkeśa smiled, and thus addressed the dejected Arjuna. The blessed Lord said: while speaking words of wisdom, you lament for that which is not to be grieved for; wise are those who do not lament

[42] *BG* 1.41–46.

> either for the living or for the dead. Never was there a time when I did not exist, nor you, nor all these kings, nor in the future shall any of us cease to exist. As childhood, youth and old age befall the soul within this body, so it comes to acquire another body; the wise one is not swayed by illusion in this matter. Heat, cold, happiness and distress – sensual perception alone produces them all, and it is impermanent, coming and going; you should seek to endure them, O Bhārata. The wise one whom these do not disturb, who thus remains even tempered in both happiness and distress, is fit for immortality, O bull among men.[43]

The values propounded here are utterly different. Kṛṣṇa does not accept the idea that prosperity in the world is good, but calls for indifference and endurance of both worldly happiness and worldly distress. These are taken to be impermanent, and to be produced by sensual perception alone. As far as being is concerned, Kṛṣṇa does not refer to the individuals present as human beings, rather he refers to them as spiritual souls or selves. In a sense, Kṛṣṇa doesn't directly answer Arjuna's doubts in regards to fighting, but performs a kind of a 'Copernical Revolution' by changing the conversation's underlying assumptions. Arjuna, on his part, argues that killing his relatives is bad; this is an obvious first-tier statement which assumes that people are subjected to death, and that death is to be avoided as far as possible for the sake of a prosperous life. Kṛṣṇa doesn't answer Arjuna's arguments, rather he shifts the conversation to a different tier or level altogether, and speaks out of different assumptions. From this higher point of view, Kṛṣṇa says that death doesn't exist at all; from his second-tier point of view, he doesn't see human beings subjected to death, rather he sees eternal spiritual souls, and as such doesn't see much logic in Arjuna's arguments. As far as values, Kṛṣṇa challenges Arjuna's idea that worldly prosperity and happiness are good and to be desired, by propounding the idea that it is indifference to both happiness and distress which is good and to be desired. Thus Kṛṣṇa speaks here out of a second-tier position.

The *Bhagavad Gītā*'s Transformational Aspects

Besides the *Bhagavad Gītā*'s theoretical aspects which may be considered in the category of *jñāna*, it has a practical side which may be considered to be in the realm of *karma*. The *Upaniṣads* and the *Brahmasūtras* are more theoretical, and as such do not offer much scope for developing a philosophy of conduct and spiritual self culture; however, the *Bhagavad Gītā* is the work in the realm of *Vedānta* that lays down the plan of life for realizing the ultimate good. This practical emphasis is not so fully present in the other two texts and, as such, without the *Bhagavad Gītā*, *Advaita*, *Viśiṣṭādvaita* and *Dvaita* would be substantially impoverished and would

---

43 *BG* 2.10–15.

lack the doctrine of the way of life.[44] As a practical scripture, the *Bhagavad Gītā* offers the means of crossing over the gap between the first tier, that of *dharma*, and the third tier, that of *mokṣa*. Mere following of *dharma* while avoiding *adharma* is not sufficient to attain the stage of *mokṣa*, but a different type of endeavour or path is needed. This process or enterprise is sometimes called 'self-realization' and it involves a transformational path by which one progresses step by step, thus making advancement from the lower tiers to the higher ones. The question may now be raised, as to what means does the *Bhagavad Gītā* offer the practitioner who desires to make progress in the process of self-realization. In other words, if the gap between *dharma* and *mokṣa* is insurmountable, how is one expected to cross it, leaving behind the world of *saṁsāra*, and attaining the liberated realm of *mokṣa*? What practical means or system does the *Bhagavad Gītā* offer the individual or the community who aspires to practice this transformative path?

A major question raised in the *Bhagavad Gītā* is whether one should choose the path of action or, alternatively, the contemplative path. This question is clearly raised twice, at the beginning of Chapters 3 and 5, and is further discussed elsewhere.[45] The *Bhagavad Gītā* clearly recommends the path of action, which offers the means by which the performer is to be elevated all the way from the tier of *dharma* to the state of *mokṣa*. This uplifting action is performed according to one's *dharma*, and continues to be carried out all along the way. Thus, Arjuna is encouraged all along his conversation with Kṛṣṇa to follow his *dharma* and fight. However, as the text progresses, he is encouraged to refine his motives for fighting; as such, the act of fighting is carried out in higher and higher inner states of consciousness. Thus, although externally one continues to carry out his prescribed duty, he undergoes an internal transformation through sublimation or purification of his motives for performing action. In this way a kind of ladder is formed, through which one rises higher and higher, from *dharma* to *mokṣa*, along the path of self-transcendence or self-realization. At the lowest stage, one's actions are motivated by simple utilitarianism,[46] and as such, one in this stage acts for the purpose of directly achieving something for himself. Underlying the following reference is the notion of 'simple utilitarianism':

> Beside that, people will be speaking of you as eternally infamous, and for one who has been honoured, dishonour is worse than death. The generals will assume that you have withdrawn from the battle out of fear, and thus, those who have once esteemed you highly will think little of you. Your ill wishers will speak many unspeakable words, thus ridiculing your capacity; what could be more distressful than this?[47]

---

44 S.S. Raghavacar, *Rāmānuja on the Gītā* (Calcutta, 1991), p. vii.

45 *BG* 3.1–3, 5.1–2, 6.1.

46 The term 'Utilitarianism' is applied here in its simple rendering, and not as a philosophical school associated with thinkers such as Bentham or Mill.

47 *BG* 2.34–36.

Here Kṛṣṇa attempts to convince Arjuna to take arms, based upon an argument underlain by simple utilitarianism. He assumes that Arjuna aspires to accumulate gain such as fame, and argues that by withdrawing from the battle, Arjuna will lose his fame. The next argument is also utilitarian, but is somewhat higher in that it accepts scriptural authority; as such it accepts the idea that warriors who die in battle attain heaven. Thus it can be named the stage of 'religious utilitarianism' or, alternatively, '*dharmic* utilitarianism'. In other words, Arjuna is advised to follow *dharma* in order to achieve some end in this life or the next:

> Happy are the *kṣatriyas* to whom such an opportunity to fight comes by good luck, as it opens heaven's gates for them.[48]

A stage still higher is following *dharma* for its own sake, or performing one's duty for the sake of duty:

> Fight for the sake of fighting, regarding alike happiness and distress, gain and loss, victory and defeat; thus you shall not incur evil.[49]

The stage of 'performing one's duty for the sake of duty' represents a pure mode of action, free from a desire for its fruits, and is one of the central teachings of the *Bhagavad Gītā*. However, it is still within the first storey as it doesn't include an awareness of the ultimate good which is, according to the *Bhagavad Gītā*, release from *saṁsāra*. Those who embody this attitude reach the top of the first tier, and can progress further into the next stage, which is already in the second tier. The next stage rejects the value of the *Vedas*, which are considered to be engaged with worldly gains, in favour of a higher ideal – the attainment of *Brahman*:

> As much value as there is in a well, when there is a flood of water on all sides, such is the value of all the *Vedas* for he who is a knower of *Brahman*.[50]

This stage may be named 'action for the sake of the highest good or *Brahman*', and one who thus acts is situated in the second tier which is characterized by various *yoga* processes. He may act now in *karma yoga*, disinterested in the fruits of his actions, and may offer those fruits to the supreme, or alternatively may practice *jñāna yoga*, *aṣṭāṅga yoga* or *bhakti yoga*. However, these various *yoga* practices have the common goal of detaching oneself from worldly existence and attachments, and attaching oneself to the supreme. The 'stage of *yoga*' is thus characterized by enlightenment and renunciation:

---

48 *BG* 2.32.

49 *BG* 2.38.

50 *BG* 2.46.

> The enlightened renounces both good and evil deeds here in this world. Therefore, perform *yoga* for the sake of *yoga*, as *yoga* is the skill in action.[51]

Having perfected the stage of *yoga*, one finally elevates himself to the third tier, that of *mokṣa*, and becomes absorbed in *Brahman*, either in an impersonal way, such as in Śaṅkara's system, or through love of the Supreme Person, such as in Rāmānuja's system. Thus the impersonal version, of 'becoming one with *Brahman*', following Śaṅkara:

> He whose happiness is within, whose pleasure is within, and his enlightenment too is within is actually a *yogī*; with his whole being absorbed in *Brahman*, he attains to extinction in *Brahman*.[52]

However, the *Bhagavad Gītā* has dominant devotional characteristics, and the loving relations to be exchanged with the personal deity, serve as a stimuli for elevation in the ethical ladder of motives, as well as the highest achievement attainable for the devoted *bhakta*, following Rāmānuja's line; thus the personal version:

> Always think of me and become my devotee, worship me and pay homage unto me; thus yoked to me and intent on me as your highest goal, you shall come to me.[53]

The stages may be summarized as simple utilitarianism, *dharmic* utilitarianism, duty for its own sake, acting for the sake of the highest good or *Brahman*, the stage of *yoga*, and the state of *mokṣa* in its personal or impersonal version. Thus an 'ethical ladder of motives' is formed, whereas the higher one's motive for action is, the higher he is situated in the *Bhagavad Gītā*'s metaphysical structure. In this way the *Bhagavad Gītā* aspires to encompass the entire realm of existence, while encouraging all to ascend the ladder of motives, thus distancing oneself from *saṁsāra* and absorbing oneself in *Brahman*, either personally or impersonally. Following this structure, I believe that the *Bhagavad Gītā* can make sense as a coherent theological-philosophical treatise, firmly tied together as a single and unified text.

---

[51] *BG* 2.50.

[52] *BG* 5.24

[53] *BG* 9.34.

Chapter 1
Setting the Scene

The Armies Ready for Battle

1 Dhṛtarāṣṭra said: O Sañjaya, what did Pāṇḍu's sons and mine do, assembled
in Kuruksetra, the field of *dharma*, eager to fight? 2 Sañjaya said: Seeing the
Pāṇḍava army arrayed for battle, king Duryodhana approached his teacher and
thus he spoke: 3 Behold, O Master, the great army of Pāṇḍu's sons, arrayed by
your excellent disciple, Drupada's son. 4 These are heroes and great archers,
equal in battle to Bhīma and Arjuna – Yuyudhāna, Virāṭa and the great warrior
Drupada. 5 Dhṛṣṭaketu, Cekitāna, the gallant king of Kāśi, Purujit, Kuntibhoja and
Śaibya, that bull among men. 6 The brave Yudhāmanyu, the valliant Uttamaujas,
the son of Subhadrā and the sons of Draupadī, each and all great warriors. 7 Now
let me name to you my outstanding army commanders, O best of the twice born.
8 These are, your honour, Bhīṣma, Karṇa, the unconquered Kṛpa, Aśvatthāman,
Vikarṇa and Somadatta's son. 9 Besides these, many other heroes are ready to
lay down their lives for my sake, all armed with various weapons and skilled in
battle. 10 Our strength protected by Bhīṣma is unlimited, whereas their strength
protected by Bhīma is limited.[1] 11 All of you in your positions, must above all
protect Bhīṣma. 12 Then, grandfather Bhīṣma, the elder of the Kurus, roared a
lion's roar and blew his conch shell, filling Duryodhana's heart with joy. 13 All
at once conches, kettledrums, cymbals, drums and trumpets were sounded in a
tremendous uproar. 14 Following that, in a great chariot drawn by white horses,
both Mādhava and Pāṇḍu's son blew their divine conches. 15 Hṛṣīkeśa blew his
conch Pāñcajanya and Dhanañjaya blew his, the Devadatta. Bhīma, whose acts
are terrible, blew his conch shell Pauṇḍra. 16 King Yudhiṣṭhira, Kuntī's son, blew
his conch called Anantavijaya, and Nakula and Sahadeva blew the Sughoṣa and
Maṇipuṣpaka. 17 The king of Kāśi, the mighty archer, Śikhaṇḍin – the celebrated
fighter, Dhṛṣṭadyumna, Virāṭa and the unconquerable Sātyaki, 18 Drupada
accompanied by Draupadī's sons, and Subhadrā's strong armed son, all blew

---

[1] Verse 11 is subject to an exegetical dispute, in regards to whose power is limited and whose is unlimited. I follow Van Buitenen who concludes that the Pāṇḍavas' power is the limited one; see J.A.B. Van Buitenen, *Studies in Indian Literature and Philosophy* (Delhi, 1988), p. 247. Radhakrishnan also translates the verse in that sense, although he reaches this conclusion differently, through translating the word '*aparyāptaṁ*' as 'unlimited' and '*paryāptaṁ*' as 'limited'. In Bhāskara's translation the verse is quoted differently, in that the names 'Bhīma' and 'Bhiṣma' are alternated, and this, too, emphasizes the Kauravas' superiority over the Pāṇḍavas. See Arvind Sharma, *The Hindu Gītā* (London, 1986), p. 18.

their conches one after the other, O Dhṛtarāṣṭra, king of the earth. 19 The conchs'
uproar made Dhṛtarāṣṭra's sons' hearts tremble, and resounded like thunder in
the sky and on the earth. 20 Then Arjuna, Hanumān on his banner, saw the sons of
Dhṛtarāṣṭra arrayed for battle; preparing for the clash of weapons he then lifted
his bow and spoke thus to Kṛṣṇa: 21–22 Arjuna said: O Acyuta, please position
the chariot between both armies, so I may behold those assembled here so eager
for battle, against whom I am to fight the impending war. 23 I desire to see those
assembled of their own will about to fight to please the evil-hearted Duryodhana.
24 Said Sañjaya: responding to Arjuna, Hṛṣīkeśa drove the fine chariot, stationing
it between the two armies. 25 In the presence of Bhīṣma, Drona, and the rulers of
the earth he said: behold, Arjuna, these Kurus assembled.

Commentary

The *Bhagavad Gītā*'s opening scene is an integral part of the *Mahābhārata*,[2] as it opens with a description of the two armies facing each other, ready for battle. As the story unfolds, it is the blind Dhṛtarāṣṭra, king of the entire dynasty and father of the Kuru commanders, who asks his assistant, Sañjaya, about the situation on the battlefield. Sañjaya, though being far from the site, sees and hears what is happening by means of special powers bestowed upon him by his *guru* Vyāsa, who also happens to be the *Mahābhārata*'s narrator. As the father of both Dhṛtarāṣṭra and his brother Pāṇḍu, Vyāsa is also the grandfather of some of the main warriors on the battlefield. In this opening scene, Duryodhana presents his army to his teacher Droṇa, and it is his opinion that his army is the superior one. At this point Arjuna, the Pāṇḍava army's commander, turns to his charioteer Kṛṣṇa, who is both his cousin and friend, and asks him to lead the fine chariot to the centre of the field, so that he can view his opponents prior to the battle's commencement.

Arjuna's Arguments Against the Fighting

26 Then Arjuna saw fathers, grandfathers, teachers, uncles, brothers, sons,
grandsons, friends, fathers in law and well wishers all standing there amidst both
armies. 27 Beholding his relatives prepared for battle, overcome by agony Arjuna
in his despondence said: 28 O Kṛṣṇa, as I look upon my relatives imbued with
fighting spirit, my limbs tremble and my mouth dries up. 29 My body quivers, my
hair stands on end, my bow Gāṇḍiva slips from my hand and my skin is afire. 30
I can no longer stand and my mind is awhirl. Only inauspicious omens do I see,
O Keśava. 31 I see no good to come from the massacre of my relatives in this
battle. O Kṛṣṇa, I desire no victory, nor the kingdom nor the happiness derived
therefrom. 32–33 O Govinda, of what use to us is the kingdom, of what use are
pleasures, or even life itself, if those for whose sake we desire kingship, pleasure

[2] The present chapter comprises the 23rd chapter of the *Bhīṣmaparvan*.

and life, are in their battle stations and have relinquished their riches and their
lives. 33–34 Teachers, fathers, sons, grandfathers, uncles, fathers in law, grandsons,
brothers in law and other kin – all these I do not wish to kill even though they may
have me slain. 35 I do not wish to kill them even for the sovereignty of the three
worlds, let alone to rule the earth. O Janārdana, having destroyed Dhṛtarāṣṭra's
sons, what joy would be left for us? 36–37 Evil only will be our lot once we slay
these aggressors. Therefore it befits us not to kill Dhṛtarāṣṭra's sons and our
own relatives. O Mādhava, having killed our own kin, what hope for happiness
remains? 38–39 O Janārdana, even if these people, their hearts overcome by greed,
see not the evil in causing the clan's destruction or in a friend's treachery, why
cannot we, who understand the wrong in a dynasty's destruction, turn our backs
to this evil? 40 With the dynasty's destruction, the eternal family *dharma* is
destroyed, and along with *dharma*'s destruction, *adharma* overpowers the entire
family. 41 When *adharma* overpowers the family its ladies become corrupt, O
Kṛṣṇa, and when the women become corrupt there is miscegenation of classes.
42 Surely miscegenation among classes leads both the clan's destroyers and the
family itself to hell. The family ancestors fall too, deprived of their due offerings
of sanctified food and water. 43 As such, the evil deeds of the destroyers which
lead to miscegenation among classes, wipe out eternal caste and family *dharma*.
44 O Janārdana, we have heard that hell awaits those whose family *dharma* has
been obliterated. 45 Alas, resolved are we on committing a great evil, if we
intend to kill our own people out of greed for royal pleasure. 46 Better had I
been killed on the battlefield, unarmed and unresisting, by Dhṛtarāṣṭra's sons
with weapons in their hands. 47 Sañjaya said: Having spoken thus on the field of
battle, Arjuna sat down upon his chariot seat, casting aside his bow and arrow,
his heart overcome with grief.

Commentary

Arjuna faces a severe crisis and has become paralysed due to conflicting values. On the one hand, his commitment to the path of the *dharma* leads him towards following the warrior's path and fighting, while on the other hand, fighting seems impossible for obvious reasons. Naturally, Arjuna wants to avoid killing his family members, confronting his teachers in battle, destroying the dynasty, acting against *dharma* and performing grave sins, deeds which may not only throw the world into chaos, but also inflict upon him suffering in future lives. Arjuna does not desire victory, a kingdom or the pleasure generated by these, and cannot see any benefit from killing his relatives; apparently, even if victory will be on his side, there would be no relatives and family members left with whom to celebrate the victory; as such, even gaining the three worlds may not be a sufficient cause for justifying such a slaughter, let alone the mere earth. Considering the reasons mentioned above, Arjuna prefers to be killed by his opponents rather than kill them. Arjuna articulates his arguments against fighting and, in doing so, lays the foundation for the dialogue with Kṛṣṇa which comprises the entire *Bhagavad Gītā*. His arguments may be divided into four:

1. The utilitarian point of view: a calculation of loss and gain shows that Arjuna will be losing by fighting rather than gaining; this argument may be further divided into simple utilitarianism and *dharmic* utilitarianism. The former calculates loss and gain directly, such as by saying that in the absence of family members, there will be no one with whom victory could be celebrated. The latter calculates loss and gain in the wider context of afterlife such as by saying that engaging in battle against the laws of *dharma* would cause Arjuna to suffer in hell in his next life.
2. Incurring evil: by fighting Arjuna would incur evil; the evil will cling to Arjuna who will not be able to rid himself of it, and as such will have to suffer its consequences in this life as well as in future lives.
3. Protecting *dharma*: fighting the battle would weaken *dharma*; as *dharma* protects the world, the weakening of *dharma* would cause the deterioration of the social order through class miscegenation, and subsequently the world would be thrown into chaos and suffering.
4. The superiority of relinquishment: Arjuna believes that he faces two options; on the one hand, active participation in worldly affairs, or on the other, relinquishment of active participation in favour of solitary introspection and spirituality. As the spiritual path is superior to worldly existence, Arjuna prefers to relinquish the battle altogether.

Having presented his arguments, Arjuna awaits Kṛṣṇa's response to his convincing arguments against fighting.

Chapter 2
The Soul, *Dharma* and Liberation

Kṛṣṇa's Rebuke of Arjuna, and Arjuna's Request for Guidance

1 Sañjaya said: Seeing the dejected Arjuna overcome by deep grief, his eyes
filled with tears, Madhusūdana spoke thus to him: 2 The blessed Lord said: How
has this dejection overcome you in this hour of crisis? It befits not the noble; not
to heaven will it lead you but to disgrace, O Arjuna. 3 Do not play the impotent,
as it befits you not; give up this base weakness of heart and rise up, O burner of
your enemies! 4 Arjuna said: O Madhusūdana, How can I shoot my arrows and
fight Bhīṣma and Droṇa as they deserve my worship? 5 It would be better to live
in this world on alms, a beggar, and not slay these noble men, my *gurus*, than
to slay these covetous *gurus* and enjoy worldly pleasures bought by their blood.
6 Nor do we know which is preferable – conquering them or being conquered
by them; Dhṛtarāṣṭra's sons, whom having killed we shall not desire to live, are
facing us arrayed for battle. 7 As my whole being is flawed and faulted by its
weakness, and my mind is confused as to the path of *dharma*, I ask you to tell me
surely which path is better? I am now your disciple and I fall at your feet; please
instruct me! 8 I can see nothing to dispel the sorrow that withers up my senses;
neither a prosperous unrivalled earthly kingdom nor even the reign of the gods.
9 Sañjaya said: Having spoken thus, Guḍākeśa, the burner of his enemies, told
Hṛṣīkeśa: Govinda, I shall not fight, and fell silent.

Commentary

Kṛṣṇa scolds Arjuna, saying that his conduct does not befit a noble. Arjuna, on his part, first considers relinquishing the battlefield altogether in order to avoid combating with his *gurus*, but then regains his composure and expresses his uncertainty as to his duty in accordance with *dharma* and the proper course to be taken. Arjuna, who has heretofore regarded Kṛṣṇa as a friend and relative, now asks Kṛṣṇa to become his *guru*, and reinforces his request by declaring his obedience. This crucial change constitutes the relationship which will henceforth underlie the conversation, a relationship in which Kṛṣṇa is the *guru* and Arjuna the disciple. Arjuna, however, is still perplexed and refuses to fight, and it is at this point that Kṛṣṇa opens his speech.

The Body and its Sensations are Temporary – the Spirit Soul is Eternal – Equanimity Leads to Immortality

> 10 O Dhṛtarāṣṭra, between both armies, Hṛsīkeśa smiled, and thus addressed the
> dejected Arjuna. 11 The blessed Lord said: while speaking words of wisdom,
> you lament for that which is not to be grieved for; wise are those who do not
> lament either for the living or for the dead. 12 Never was there a time when I
> did not exist, nor you, nor all these kings, nor in the future shall any of us cease
> to exist. 13 As childhood, youth and old age befall the soul within this body,
> so it comes to acquire another body; the wise one is not swayed by illusion
> in this matter. 14 Heat, cold, happiness and distress – sensual perception alone
> produces them all, and it is impermanent, coming and going; you should seek to
> endure them, O Bhārata. 15 The wise one whom these do not disturb, who thus
> remains even tempered in both happiness and distress, is fit for immortality, O
> bull among men.

Commentary

Although Arjuna seems to speak authoritatively, he is in fact unwise as he grieves over that which is not to be grieved upon, namely the advent of death. The reason for this is that the spiritual soul passes in this body from childhood to old age, and then passes to the next body at the time of death. Kṛṣṇa exemplifies this principle by pointing at himself, at Arjuna and at the assembled kings, and says that all of them have always existed and will always exist. Kṛṣṇa illustrates the passage of the soul from one body to another by describing how it proceeds from one bodily form into another already in this lifetime; as such, the soul transmigrates from the child's body into the adult's body, and yet again into the old man's body, before it finally leaves to accept a new body. A truly wise man understands this and is therefore not troubled by the occurrence of death, which is but a natural outcome of the embodied condition. In describing the body–soul relationship, Kṛṣṇa expresses himself through a different terminology than Arjuna's; by declaring that the various bodily states befall the soul encaged within the body, he articulates himself through a 'second tier terminology', a mode of discourse which denotes subjective and individual reality to the soul alone as opposed to the human being as a whole. Kṛṣṇa looks into the happiness and the distress with which Arjuna is overwhelmed; these too are nothing but a transient and external sense perception, just like the sentient body experiencing them, and are not the experience of the soul. As such, Arjuna is advised to develop indifference towards them and subsequently attain eternal life. In addressing Arjuna, Kṛṣṇa invalidates Arjuna's arguments by pointing at their weak underlying assumptions, and raises the discussion to a higher level or dimension. Applying the three-tier model, Arjuna's various arguments would be categorized as belonging to the 'first tier', as these perceive the human being as a complete subjective individual whose aim is to prosper in this world. As such, Arjuna considers himself to be a warrior whose duty is to follow *dharma* for the betterment of the world. Kṛṣṇa's arguments, however, are articulated from a 'second tier' position; accordingly the subjective individual is the eternal and conscious spiritual soul, whose aim is the attainment of release from this world through enduring both happiness and distress. This introduction to Kṛṣṇa's speech indicates to a large extent the course of the entire treatise, as these ideas, presently introduced in but a preliminary manner, require extension and further clarification. The eternal soul, the transition from body to body, happiness and distress, the senses and the body, liberation and eternal life – all these will engage Kṛṣṇa and Arjuna in their following discussion. As such, Chapter 2 constitutes to a large extent a summary of the entire *Bhagavad Gītā*, referring in a concise manner to various ideas which will be expanded upon in later chapters.

The Nature of the Soul

> 16 There is no becoming of the unreal, there is no unbecoming for the real; the seers of the truth have reached both conclusions. 17 Know that to be indestructible, by which everything is pervaded; there is none who can destroy the imperishable. 18 For these bodies the end is sure, whereas that which is embodied in them, the indestructible and immeasurable soul, is said to be eternal. Therefore, O Bhārata, fight! 19 He who deems the soul is the slayer, and he who thinks the soul is slain – both of them do not know, for the soul slays not nor is it slain. 20 The soul is never born, nor does it ever die; nor having come into existence, will it ever cease to be. Unborn, eternal, unending and primeval – it is not killed when the body is killed. 21 The person who knows the soul as eternally imperishable, that it was not born and is indestructible – whom does he kill? Whom does he cause to kill? 22 As one, having cast aside his old and worn garments, takes on other new ones, so the embodied soul, having cast aside its worn and old bodies, takes on other new ones. 23 Weapons do not pierce it, fire does not burn it, water does not wet it and wind does not parch it. 24 The soul cannot be cut, it cannot be burned, it cannot be wetted or dried indeed, for it is eternal, all pervading, stable, fixed and primeval. 25 It is said that the soul is not manifested, it is inconceivable and beyond transformation; therefore, having understood the matter in that way, you should not grieve. 26 Moreover, if you assume that it is continually born or continually dies, you still have no reason to lament, O mighty warrior. 27 Death is inevitable for all that is born, and inevitable is rebirth for the dead; therefore, you should not grieve over the inevitable. 28 Beings are not manifested in their beginnings, are manifest as they continue to exist, and not manifested at their end; therefore, O Bhārata, why lament about it? 29 For someone to see it is a wonder, for someone else to speak of it is a wonder, for another to hear of it is a wonder, and even having heard of it, no one understands. 30 The soul within everyone's body is beyond destruction; therefore, you should not mourn for any living being.

Commentary

The nature of the soul is implicitly contrasted with that of the body; the soul is eternal and primeval, it is not subjected to birth nor to death, it changes bodies just as one changes garments, it is wondrous, difficult to comprehend, permanent and unchanging. As opposed to the soul, which cannot be harmed by fire, water or weapons, the body is transient and mortal by nature. The sharp distinction between the body and the soul is also expressed through terming the soul 'the body's owner',[1] an expression which hints at a situation in which the owner exists in a bodiless state, i.e. the state of immortality or liberation.[2]

Justifying the War by Means of Utilitarianism, *Dharmic* Utilitarianism and *Dharma* for it's Own Sake

> 31 Considering your own duty, you should not hesitate, as there is indeed nothing better for a *kṣatriya* than fighting a *dharmic* war. 32 Happy are the *kṣatriyas* to whom such an opportunity to fight comes by good luck, as it opens heaven's gates for them. 33 If, however, you will not fight this *dharmic* war, you will be giving up both your *dharma* and honour, and so incur evil. 34 Beside that, people will be speaking of you as eternally infamous, and for one who has been honoured, dishonour is worse than death. 35 The generals will assume that you have withdrawn from the battle out of fear, and thus, those who have once esteemed you highly will think little of you. 36 Your ill wishers will speak many unspeakable words, thus ridiculing your capacity; what could be more distressful than this? 37 Either you will be killed and attain heaven, or, having conquered, you will enjoy the earth. Therefore arise, Kaunteya, resolute for battle! 38 Fight for the sake of fighting, regarding alike happiness and distress, gain and loss, victory and defeat; thus you shall not incur evil.

Commentary

Having rejected Arjuna's position through 'second-tier arguments', Kṛṣṇa now descends back to the 'first tier' and addresses Arjuna from his own point of view which is somewhat more worldly. Kṛṣṇa now refers to Arjuna as a *kṣatriya* who knows the codes of *dharma*, and systematically presents various arguments as to why Arjuna should fight. Arjuna sees inauspicious omens, and considers that no possible good would result from killing his relatives;[3] to this Kṛṣṇa replies that fighting can only be advantageous to Arjuna, since he will earn this world's kingdom in case he wins, and the heavenly world in case he gets

---

1 *Dehin*, see verse 22.

2 Already indicated in verse 15.

3 *BG* 1.30–31.

killed in the battle.[4] Arjuna claims that by fighting he would incur evil,[5] and Kṛṣṇa answers that the opposite is true, since if he withdraws from the battle thereby neglecting his duty, he will then be incurring evil.[6] Arjuna asks how can the death of relatives bring joy,[7] and Kṛṣṇa replies that happy are the *kṣatriyas* to whom such an opportunity for *dharmic* combat comes by good fortune.[8] Arjuna considers the fighting to be contrary to *dharma*,[9] while Kṛṣṇa considers refraining from fighting to be contrary to *dharma*.[10] Arjuna fears to wind up in hell,[11] whereas Kṛṣṇa promises him a dwelling on the earth or heaven.[12] In essence, Kṛṣṇa presents three arguments:

1. By refraining from fighting, Arjuna will suffer dishonour, since the generals will consider him a coward abandoning the battle out of fear. Since honour is preferable to dishonour, it is advisable for Arjuna to fight. Underlying this argument is a simple calculation of loss and gain and, as such, it may be characterized as representing the stage of 'simple utilitarianism'; this is the lowest stage of the 'ethical ladder of self-transcendence'.
2. According to the principles of *dharma*, warriors killed in fighting a *dharmic* war attain heaven. Therefore, if Arjuna wins, he will win the earthly kingdom and if he is killed, he will win the heavenly kingdom; as such, Arjuna will be gaining either way. This argument is somewhat more sophisticated then the previous one, as it requires faith in the principles of *dharma*, i.e. faith that by dying in a *dharmic* war, one attains heaven. As it is still based upon utilitarianism, it may be considered '*dharmic* utilitarianism' and it comprises the second stage of the 'ethical ladder'.
3. Arjuna must follow his duty for its own sake, adhere to his *dharmic* duty regardless of calculations of a utilitarian nature and fight for the sake of fighting. He should be indifferent to the outcome of the battle and not aspire for any sort of gain; by fighting in this frame of mind he will avoid committing evil. This argument is beyond utilitarianism as the fulfilment of the duty in itself comprises success, disregarding external success or failure. This stage is still higher than the previous one and may be considered 'adhering to *dharma* for its own sake'.

---

4 *BG* 2.37.

5 *BG* 1.36–37.

6 *BG* 2.33.

7 *BG* 1.35–37.

8 *BG* 2.32.

9 *BG* 1.40–44.

10 *BG* 2.33.

11 *BG* 1.44.

12 *BG* 2.37.

The two lower stages are motivated by a desire for gain and, as such, are not free from evil. In the third position, however, one does not desire gain but only the adherence to duty for its own sake, and as such it is free from evil. It therefore seems that to the degree one is free from desire, he is free from involvement with evil.

From *Dharma* to *Mokṣa*

> 39 This enlightenment has been described to you through *Sāṅkhya* or theory;
> now please hear of it through *yoga* or practice, for, once absorbed in this
> enlightenment, you shall free yourself from the bondage of *karma*. 40 In this
> effort there is no loss, nor is there any reversal to be found; even a little of this
> *dharma* protects one from great fear. 41 O Arjuna, enlightenment in this world
> depends on a single-minded resolute nature; by contrast, the intelligence of the
> irresolute is many-branched, indeed endless. 42–43 O Pārtha, the unwise who take
> pleasure in words of the *Veda*, say that there is nothing beyond these flowery
> and delightful words, which give good *karma*, good birth and good fruits of
> action. Full of desires and with heaven as their aim, these people practice an
> abundance of rituals, with the purpose of achieving pleasure and power. 44 Those
> attached to pleasure and power thus have their thoughts and insight stolen away;
> therefore, the resolute determination and enlightenment to be found in the state
> of *samādhi*, do not come to them. 45 The *Vedas* have the world of the three
> *guṇas* as their domain; O Arjuna, rise above the three *guṇas*' realm! Be free from
> duality, always planted in the truth, free from the desire to possess and preserve,
> and established in the self. 46 As much value as there is in a well, when there is
> a flood of water on all sides, such is the value of all the *Vedas* for he who is a
> knower of *Brahman*. 47 Your sole entitlement is to perform *dharmic* activity, not
> ever to possess its fruits; never shall the fruit of an action motivate your deed,
> and never cleave to inaction. 48 O Dhanañjaya, perform activities while you are
> fixed in *yoga*; relinquishing attachment, be equally accepting of both success
> and failure, for this equanimity is called *yoga*. 49 Action is far inferior to *buddhi*
> *yoga* or enlightened action, Arjuna. Seek refuge in this enlightenment, as those
> motivated by the fruits of their actions are to be pitied. 50 The enlightened person
> renounces both good and evil deeds here in this world; therefore, perform *yoga*
> for its own sake, as *yoga* is the skill in action. 51 The wise who are rooted in
> this enlightenment relinquish indeed the fruits born of actions; thus they are
> freed from the bondage of rebirth, and go to that place which is free from any
> pain. 52 When your consciousness has made its way through the dense tangle of
> delusion, you shall become averse to all that has been heard, and all that is to be
> heard (in the *Vedas*). 53 When you will be fixed and unwavering in the face of the
> perplexing *Vedic* hymns, your consciousness fixed in unshaken *samādhi*, then
> you will have attained to the state of *yoga*.

Commentary

This section opens with Kṛṣṇa's statement that so far the subject of enlightenment has been described through *Sāṅkhya* or theory; this seems to refer to the elaborate description of the soul and the implicit idea of liberation from the embodied state. The discussion was mainly ontological in that it was occupied with the question of 'what is that which exists'? The answer was that it is eternal souls imprisoned in bodies that exist. The discussion now turns to engage with the same subject matter of enlightenment, but this time from a different point of view, i.e. the point of view of action; as such, the discussion is now deontological, and is concerned with the manner of performing duty or activity. Thus the question under discussion now is 'how should one act'? These two approaches are found in the *Bhagavad Gītā* side by side and their purpose is the same – liberation. Apparently, a comparison of the two approaches is required; this indeed takes place later twice where the question regarding which of the two is superior – knowledge or action – is raised and discussed.[13] Two types of persons are dichotomized and their state of mind examined; on the one hand, there are those who strive for enlightenment and on the other hand, those aiming at worldly pleasures in this life and the next. Those whose aim is enlightenment possess inner resolution, and the efforts they make on their way to enlightenment are not in vain, since they continue to advance life after life, and proceed from the point reached in their former life. As opposed to those striving for enlightenment there are others who are engaged in pursuing success in the world, through the splendid *Vedic* sacrifices, and whose aim is the acquisition of higher planets, good birth and the satisfaction of sensual desires. Their adherence to *dharma* is derived from considerations of utility and gain, since for them *dharma* is the means for achieving worldly aims. These people lack inner determination since their intelligence is confused by the abundance of desires which they seek to gratify. Moreover, they claim that there is nothing higher than satiating these desires.

It seems that although Kṛṣṇa has addressed Arjuna's various concerns, the issue of evil has remained unresolved. Kṛṣṇa has provided two reasons for fighting, and these are 'simple utilitarianism' and '*dharmic* utilitarianism'; these two positions are flawed, in that acting in this manner involves evil and, as a consequence, future suffering. Kṛṣṇa has also offered Arjuna a third, higher reason for fighting and that is '*dharma* for its own sake'; this position does offer a solution to the problem as by acting in this manner, one is freed from evil. Apparently this idea requires a further elaboration, and this elaboration is offered in the present section; it seems that the realm of evil is the 'first tier', where one aims at worldly prosperity, but that evil is absent from the realm of the 'second tier', where one aims at liberation. As the 'first tier' involves evil, one is obliged to follow the injunctions of *dharma* in order to avoid it, whereas the 'second tier' does not involve evil, and as such, one situated at this level is exempt from following *dharmic* injunctions, although

---

[13] *BG* 3.1–8, 5.1–6.

he may follow these injunctions for the sake of giving example to the general mass of people.[14] A possible conclusion of this discussion is that evil is inevitable in the case of an action performed with an interest in its fruits, and therefore the only way to avoid evil is to act without regards to the fruits of action.

The subject of liberated enlightenment is introduced here; knowledge of *Brahman*, liberation and release from the world of *saṁsāra* are grouped and contrasted with the *Vedic* sacrifices which aim at enjoyment in this life and the next. The new state described herein is a state of *yoga*, enlightenment,[15] *samādhi* and knowledge of *Brahman*. It seems that this section presents a preliminary discussion which does not differentiate these four concepts, rather takes them to be more or less synonymous, emphasizing that the path leading to them is worthwhile as it delivers one from *saṁsāra*. The enlightened state involves liberation from the bonds of *karma* or the reaction to actions, and is placed above the scope of the three *guṇas*. This state requires indifference to the world along with its good and bad alike. Whoever has achieved it is a master of action, and that state leads to freedom from the bonds of birth and death, and to delivery from suffering. The attack on the *Vedas* may be surprising; why is Kṛṣṇa so critical of the *Vedas*, and why now? It may be that the criticism is directed towards *Vedic* schools such as the *Mīmāmsā*, a school which is somewhat cynical towards questions of liberation and enlightenment. It seems that the *Vedas* not only represent divinity but endorse and justify the utilitarian concept of *dharma*; also, the *Vedas* are confined to the domain of three *guṇas*, and hence another reason to transcend them. As Arjuna is being encouraged to relinquish the utilitarian mentality, he is encouraged to give up the *Vedas*, at least in their ritualistic emphasis which is inspired by a desire for various fruits. As a substitute Kṛṣṇa proposes a different ideal of impersonal divinity, namely *Brahman*, a term associated with the *Upaniṣadic* world. This tension between the *Vedic* and the *Upaniṣadic* worlds is fundamental to the *Bhagavad Gītā*, and as the *Bhagavad Gītā* favours the *Upaniṣadic* worldview, it is sometimes called *Gītopaniṣad*.

This section includes decrees, the best known of which is verse 47: one is entitled to *dharmic* action alone, but not to its fruits; nor shall the fruits of action become the source of inspiration for one's deeds, and at the same time one should not become inactive by giving up action altogether. To that end one must find another motive for activity, namely enlightenment; as such, one whose aim is enlightenment should follow *dharma* in a disinterested state of mind and without regards to the fruits of his endeavours. This suggests that *dharma* serves as an external framework while internally one aims at enlightenment and liberation. The idea of following '*dharma* for its own sake' for the purpose of avoiding evil involves a paradox; after all, the reason for avoiding evil is to avoid the consequence of suffering, and apparently, one who acts in this way is not indifferent to both happiness and distress. Therefore, a different state which is above the realm of

---

[14] This theme will be further discussed in Chapter 3; see *BG* 3.21–26.

[15] *Buddhi*.

both happiness and distress is to be provided and it is located not in the conceptual domain of the first tier but in that of the second one.[16] This state is 'being fixed in *buddhi yoga*',[17] and only in that position can one truly act without regards to the fruits of action. The outcome is a new and higher state of existence, namely, action of which the purpose is the highest good such as enlightenment and the attainment of *Brahman*. This is a higher state than following *dharma* for its own sake, and it can be classified as the fourth step in the ladder.

The Steady Enlightenment

> 54 Arjuna asked: He who is established in steady enlightenment, and situated in
> *samādhi*, O Keśava – How can he be described? That enlightened one – how
> does he speak? How does he sit, and how does he walk? 55 The Blessed Lord
> said: When he forsakes all desires arising from the mind, becomes satisfied in the
> self and by the self alone, then he is said to have attained steady enlightenment.
> 56 One not agitated despite all kinds of distress, whose aspiration for happiness is
> gone, and who is devoid of passion, fear and anger – such a sage is said to have
> attained steady enlightenment. 57 He who is not attracted to anything, and having
> attained this or that, good or bad, does not rejoice but is not averse either – his
> wisdom is firmly established. 58 When one is able to withdraw his senses away
> from their objects under any circumstance, just as a tortoise withdraws its limbs
> into the shell – his wisdom is firmly established. 59 When the embodied abstains
> – the objects of the senses fade away, but the taste for them remains; however,
> even the taste fades away, when one attains the vision of the Supreme.

Commentary

Kṛṣṇa has defined the concept of steady enlightenment as a solution for the problem of evil and as an ideal to be aspired to; Arjuna now wishes to learn more about this state, and asks about the characteristics of one who has reached that ideal position. In reply, Kṛṣṇa describes the enlightened as indifferent to the external world, while experiencing an inner satisfaction and a vision of the supreme. The external indifference is achieved after restraining the senses, which the enlightened withdraws just like the tortoise withdraws its limbs. Following the sensual withdrawal and the attainment of the vision of the supreme, the taste for sensual experiences disappears. A further stage of the ladder is being unveiled: a state in which one experiences internal satisfaction attained after restraining the senses

[16] The text hints at a position higher still than the second tier in verse 51: 'that place which is freed from any pain' may be taken to be the state of *mokṣa*, or the third tier according to our model.

[17] *Buddhi*: enlightenment, wisdom. *Yoga*: connecting, linking or yoking to a higher state of existence.

and developing indifference to the external world. This state clearly represents the second tier, since one is already deeply absorbed in the process of liberation, and it will be further developed in the following section. The text proceeds to expand the discussion on the subject of the senses.

The Turbulent Senses and the State of Perfection

> 60 Although the wise may strive to control his mind, the turbulent senses
> nevertheless forcibly carry it away. 61 Having controlled all the senses, being
> yoked to me and intent on me as the Supreme – he who has firm control of his
> senses in that way – his wisdom is firmly established. 62 When one contemplates
> the objects of the senses, an attachment for them arises; from attachment springs
> desire, and from desire anger is born. 63 Anger yields delusion, and delusion
> bewilders the memory; bewilderment of memory causes a loss of intelligence,
> and when the intelligence is lost, one is ruined. 64 But when his senses dwell
> in their objects devoid of attraction or repulsion, being self-controlled and
> following scriptural injunctions, he then obtains the divine grace. 65 Having
> obtained the divine grace, all miseries cease to exist for him. With his heart
> tranquil, quickly does he attain steady enlightenment. 66 For him who is not
> yoked, there is no enlightenment, and without enlightenment there can be no
> contemplation of the self; without contemplation there can be no peace. How
> can one who is not at peace be happy? 67 The mind that follows the wandering
> senses carries away the intelligence just as a wind carries away a boat on the
> sea. 68 Therefore, O mighty Arjuna, he who restrains his senses and keeps them
> entirely away from their objects – his wisdom is firm indeed. 69 That which is
> night for all beings is the time of awakening for the man of restraint; when all
> beings are awake, that time is night for the visionary sage. 70 Although rivers
> constantly fill the ocean, it nevertheless remains unmoved; similarly, he attains
> peace, who remains unmoved although desires intrude, and not he who lusts
> to satisfy them. 71 Casting aside all desires, one who is free from aspiration,
> possessiveness and egotism attains peace. 72 This is the state of *Brahman*, O
> Pārtha; having once attained this state, one is no longer subject to illusion; being
> thus fixed, he reaches extinction in *Brahman* even at the hour of death.

Commentary

This chapter which has begun with Arjuna's arguments against fighting, has gradually developed into a presentation of a complete worldview involving a description of the embodied soul, a rejection of utilitarian modes of action, and the establishment of liberation from the world of *saṁsāra* as the goal to be sought after. Now, that the ideal has been established the main obstacle for achieving this ideal is to be discussed too, and this is the topic of the senses and sensual attraction. This section, therefore, elaborates on the topic of sense restraint and its relation to enlightenment; in view of the importance of this subject matter, the central ideas are articulated:

1. One fixed in steady enlightenment is capable of withdrawing his senses from their objects as the turtle draws his limbs into his shell.[18]
2. The senses carry away one's mind, even though he may be wise and strives to restrain them.[19]
3. Desires arise by mentally contemplating sense objects.[20]
4. When the mind follows the wandering senses, it carries the intelligence away, as the wind carries away a boat in the sea.[21]
5. The state of enlightenment requires restrained senses and indifference to desires.[22]
6. One who is free from passions attains peace.[23]

Although the soul is not explicitly mentioned in this section, its presence is implicit and it could be added to the various mental and gross components mentioned for the purpose of constructing the *Yogic-Upaniṣadic* concept of the human being. The struggle with the senses could thus be deconstructed into its various components, and there seems to be a kind of 'tug of war' in which each side pulls in its own direction; the senses on their part pull towards their objects, drawing the mind, which draws the intelligence, which draws the embodied soul. From the other side, the individual subject desiring release is the soul, which draws the intelligence, which draws the mind which tries to restrain the senses and enable the soul to progress towards liberation. This idea is well illustrated in the *Upaniṣadic* 'chariot metaphor';[24] accordingly, the chariot represents the body, the passenger represents the self or the soul, the charioteer represents the intellect, the reins represent the mind and the five horses represent the five senses. When the passenger is in command of the charioteer, who in turn firmly holds the reins and restrains the horses, the chariot proceeds safely towards the desired destination. However, when the horses are out of control and pull the chariot towards whimsical directions, the reins fall out of the charioteer's grip, and the chariot along with the passenger faces danger. When the senses are victorious, a chain of events occurs, leading to the destruction of the attempt to get released from this world, and consequently one falls back again into *saṁsāra*.[25] As one occurrence in the chain of events leads to another,

---

[18] 2.58.

[19] 2.60.

[20] 2.62.

[21] 2.67.

[22] 2.70–71.

[23] 2.71.

[24] *Kaṭha Upaniṣad*, 3.3–9.

[25] 'Destruction' is derived from the term *praṇaśyati* (2.63) translated as 'is lost', and describes the end of the causal succession of events starting with contemplating the objects

it is causal, and it is composed of eight stages;[26] it begins with the contemplation of sense objects, subsequently attachment for them arises, desire follows and this results in anger. Anger is followed by delusion which is followed by forgetfulness, and this causes the loss of intelligence and subsequently one falls into *saṁsāra* and is thus ruined. This reminds one of the similar Buddhist causal chain called *pratītya samutpāda* or 'dependent origination', composed of 12 stages, beginning with ignorance and resulting in old age and death. As opposed to the unrestrained who is vanquished, the victorious soul who is able to restrain the senses, the mind and its desires, becomes subsequently indifferent to external desires and gains inner peace. Kṛṣṇa openly encourages Arjuna to strive for enlightenment while rejecting passions, and offers himself as an object of meditation.[27] By now, the fifth level of the 'ethical ladder' has been articulated; this is the state of inner bliss and serenity, which appears after rejecting the senses and concentrating on the supreme. This state is higher than the previous one since, in the fourth stage, one strives to achieve *Brahman*, but in the present stage, one gets closer to *Brahman* and this is verified by the experience of inner bliss. The state of inner bliss may also be taken as a reply to Arjuna who asks 'having killed our own kin, what happiness will be left for us'?[28] The answer received is that the inner happiness described here will be left for Arjuna, having made internal progress and achieved the stage of inner happiness. In summary of this chapter, much has been stated so far, and the agenda for the entire *Bhagavad Gītā* has been set; at this stage, the first and second tiers have been encountered, and five stages of the 'ethical ladder' have been revealed. This chapter is in a large part an epitome of the whole treatise, and many of the ideas briefly mentioned so far will be further developed later on. Henceforth the reading of the text will be easier and less intense.

---

of the senses. The expression is undoubtedly sharp, but seems to fit the spirit of the text as contemplating the sense objects throws the soul deep into *saṁsāra*. This fall is described as a 'great fear' (2.40).

[26] 2.62–63.

[27] 2.61.

[28] *BG* 1.35–37.

Chapter 3

The Path of Enlightened Action – Part I

What is Better – Enlightenment or Action?

1 Arjuna said: O Janārdana, if you consider enlightenment to be better than
action, why then do you enjoin me to perform this terrible act? 2 Your equivocal
like words confuse my mind; I beg you, make me certain of one thing, by which
I may attain the best. 3 The blessed Lord said: I have propounded since the days
of yore, O Blameless Arjuna, that in this world there are two paths; for those
who uphold reasoning, it is the path of *jñāna* or intellectual *yoga*, whereas for
those who uphold action, the path of *karma yoga*, or *yoga* of activity exists. 4
Not merely by abstaining from acting does one attain actionlessness, and not
by renunciation alone does one achieve perfection. 5 No one, indeed, can ever
refrain entirely from acting even for a moment, for everyone is helplessly driven
to action by the *guṇas* born of material nature. 6 He who restrains his active
organs, but nevertheless contemplates the sense objects within his mind, is held
to be a self-deceiving hypocrite. 7 Superior, however, is he who restrains his
senses by the mind, and at the same time in a detached fashion engages his
organs and performs *karma yoga*. 8 Perform your *dharmic* duty, as action is
superior to inaction; even in maintaining your body you cannot succeed without
embracing action.

Commentary

The third chapter opens with Arjuna's question as to what is preferable: action or enlightenment. Arjuna is justly perplexed; in describing the soul, Kṛṣṇa has spoken from the viewpoint of the path of knowledge,[1] and subsequently spoken from the viewpoint of the path of action,[2] as clearly indicated.[3] Nevertheless, the subject remained equivocal, as Kṛṣṇa has described knowledge of *Brahman* to be higher than the *Vedic* sacrifices which further action.[4] He has described the ideal state of action as a state of enlightenment or *Buddhi*.[5] Moreover, he has emphasized the fact that the ideal person is indifferent to both good and evil

---

1 *BG* 2.12–30.
2 *BG* 2.47.
3 *BG* 2.39.
4 *BG* 2.46.
5 *BG* 2.49.

deeds.[6] It seems that by all this Kṛṣṇa suggests that Arjuna renounce the world to become a *sannyāsin*, an idea already proposed previously by Arjuna himself.[7] At the same time, Arjuna and Kṛṣṇa are situated in the battlefield, where Kṛṣṇa urges Arjuna to lead his army into a battle which will no doubt result in a massive massacre. Arjuna therefore requests Kṛṣṇa to define his position unequivocally: spirituality or fighting. Underlying Arjuna's question is the assumption that the path of action involves actively adhering to *dharma* for the purpose of establishing a moral and prosperous human society, whereas the path of enlightenment seems to be radically different. As such, Arjuna considers the path of enlightenment to involve the relinquishment of active participation in worldly affairs, in favour of quiet contemplation and the practice of austerity aimed at *mokṣa* or liberation from the world altogether. In his reply, though, Kṛṣṇa seems to be thinking in different categories; he doesn't seem to accept this dichotomy between action and enlightenment, or between the values of *dharma* and the values of *mokṣa*, rather he considers both action and enlightenment to be paths leading to *mokṣa*. From his point of view, both are *yogic* paths which lead one to the supreme, but whereas the former emphasizes action the latter emphasizes contemplation. As such, the path of action leads to ultimate liberation through the active adherence to *dharma*, whereas the path of knowledge leads to liberation through the intellectual study of metaphysics and the cultivation of true knowledge of the soul and its relationships with *Brahman*. Hence Kṛṣṇa refers to these two as the path of action or *karma yoga* and the path of knowledge or *jñāna yoga*; he contrasts the path of action with the path of knowledge, and while endorsing the path of knowledge as commendable, he recommends the path of action as preferable. Kṛṣṇa argues that since one is driven to act helplessly, being compelled to do so by the *guṇas*, it is preferable for him to act in *karma yoga* and thereby turn this state of constant activity into a *yogic* practice. This is better than practicing extraneous asceticism for the purpose of detachment and the quiet contemplation of the highest truth, while at the same time contemplating the objects of the senses within the mind, due to the constant mental disturbance caused by the *guṇas*.

Kṛṣṇa justifies his preference for disciplined *yogic* action – *karma yoga*, by different arguments. He claims that it is impossible to cease from acting, and that one is ultimately helpless as activity is forced upon him by the three *guṇas*; furthermore, even the maintenance of the body is not possible without at least some activity. As such, he argues, if one is anyhow going to act, he might as well act in *karma yoga* and employ his actions for the purpose of spiritual upliftment, rather than be driven to act helplessly under the *guṇas*' control. Having made this argument, Kṛṣṇa presents a new ideal, namely actionlessness. Inactivity and actionlessness appear to differ, since activity and inactivity relate to bodily and mental activity or its absence, while action and actionlessness relate to the creation of *karma* or to the absence of its creation. Accordingly, in the state of

---

6 *BG* 2.50.

7 *BG* 1.45.

action there is a chain of reactions generated and these cause one a continuous entanglement in *saṁsāra*. Conversely, in the state of actionlessness there is no chain of reactions generated despite factual action. The example is given of one who aspires to actionlessness, but attempts to achieve it in the wrong way; he avoids action externally and appears to be an ascetic, while at the same time his thoughts turn to the objects of his senses, to which he is attached. This kind of a person is labelled as a hypocrite and a confused soul, and in contrast the positive example of the ideal person acting in *karma yoga* is established. This ideal person initiates bodily activity while performing his *dharmic* duty, not out of a desire to reap the fruits of his deeds, but as a way to engage his body in activity under the injunctions of *dharma*, and with the aid of his mind he controls his senses and organs of action. Such control is not an attempt to prevent the senses and bodily organs from acting altogether, but is an activity destined to keep them on the right path, just as a coachman controls his horses so that they do not depart from the road but proceed solely in the right direction. This position is preferred by Kṛṣṇa, and it includes some elements generally associated with the path of *jñāna yoga* as well; it is reflexive since one conceives his body to be an instrument distinct from himself. Also, the body is taken to be different than the soul in that it is subject to certain external rules, namely the influence of the *guṇas*, which do not necessarily express the soul's will directly. This position is an expansion of the vision articulated by Kṛṣṇa in the second chapter, in which he described the soul or the self as different from the body.[8] In summary, the difference between the path of knowledge and the path of action has been preliminarily discussed in the second chapter, and has been further developed here. The two paths have been compared and the path of action or *karma yoga* was recommended as preferable and more suitable than the path knowledge or *jñāna yoga*. As such, Kṛṣṇa's position is that Arjuna must fight as a practice of *karma yoga*.

The Importance of Sacrifice

> 9 The whole world is bound by action save for action that has sacrifice as its aim.[9] Free from attachment, perform action for that purpose, O Kaunteya. 10 In ancient times, Prajāpati, the lord of beings created them along with sacrifices and told them: may you prosper by this! Let this be your cow to yield all desires! 11 May you please the gods herein, and may the gods please you. Thus, pleasing one another, you shall attain the highest good. 12 Being pleased by the sacrifice, the gods will bestow upon you the desired pleasures, but he who enjoys their gifts without an offering in return is a thief.[10] 13 Good people who eat the remnants of

8 *BG* 2.12–30.

9 The term *yajña* is translated as sacrifice although it can also be taken to be a name for Viṣṇu; the latter translation would naturally render the verse a more devotional purport.

10 The root *Bhu* taken as 'to please'.

> the sacrifice are absolved from all evils; wicked people, however, who cook for their own sake, verily eat only evil. 14 All living beings subsist on food, and food is produced by the rain; rain falls as a result of sacrifice, and sacrifice originates from *dharmic* activity. 15 *Dharmic* activity is born of *Brahman* which is in the *Veda*, and *Brahman* springs from the eternal Oṁ. Therefore, the all pervading *Brahman* is eternally present in the sacrifice. 16 He who does not keep turning the sacrificial wheel thus set in motion, lives an evil life while indulging in the senses and indeed, O Pārtha, he lives in vain.

Commentary

The previous section has ended with Arjuna being enjoined to carry out *dharmic* duty;[11] Kṛṣṇa now expands this by emphasizing the central role sacrifice occupies in the *dharmic* worldview. Accordingly, sacrifice was created at the beginning of creation along with human beings, and it is instrumental for attaining prosperity. Underlying the idea of sacrifice is the reciprocity between humans and gods, as when one offers the gods various goods in sacrifice, they are pleased and grant him their blessings in return. He then offers some of the abundance provided back to them, and when this circular process is repeated time and again, it becomes the sacrificial wheel. *Brahman* too is represented in the act of sacrifice, since sacrifice originates in *dharma*, *dharma* originates in the *Vedas* and the *Vedas* originate in *Brahman*. A question may be raised: how is it that Kṛṣṇa supports sacrifice, having condemned it in the previous chapter,[12] and having denounced those performing *Vedic* sacrifices by calling them unintelligent? Despite that, the present section recommends sacrifice as the way for living a pious life, and as the means of being released from evil. As such, one may justly ask; what has changed? It appears that the nature of the sacrifice described here differs from the *Vedic* sacrifices previously mentioned. The sacrifices previously described were performed for the purpose of enjoying this world and the next; as such, their performance represents the second step in the ethical ladder of values, i.e. of following *dharma* in order to gain some fruits. The sacrifice described here is performed for the purpose of attaining the supreme good; this is certainly a higher motive and it represents the fourth step in the ethical ladder. The adherence to *dharma* is also considered to be a sacrifice and, as such, Arjuna is encouraged to follow his duty and fight as a sacrificial performance. This offers a further development of the previous section; since Arjuna must act anyway, it is preferable for him to act according to *dharma* so that his activity will become a sacrifice, rather than act for his personal satisfaction. This is so because while ordinarily activity is touched by evil and binds one through the chains of *karma*, sacrificial activity whose aim is *Brahman* does not.[13] As such, following *dharma* can only be to Arjuna's advantage; not only

---

[11] *BG* 3.8.

[12] *BG* 2.42–45.

[13] As opposed to sacrificial activity aimed at enjoying its fruits, such as in *BG* 2.42–43.

will he satisfy his desires and live a pious life, but he will also be released from evil and will attain the supreme good.

The Enlightened One is Free from *Dharma's* Injunctions

> 17 But for one who is delighted in the self alone, and is thus self-satisfied and self-content indeed, for him – no *dharmic* duty exists. 18 He has no interest to perform any action, but no reason to avoid action either. He needs not depend on any creature. 19 Therefore, ever perform your duties while detached, as one who does so disinterestedly indeed attains the Supreme. 20 By adhering to *dharmic* duty alone have Janaka and others attained success; considering the welfare of the world, you should do likewise. 21 Whatever a great man does, common men indeed follow, and whatever standard he sets, the whole world accepts. 22 O Pārtha, I myself am not obliged to perform any duty in all the three worlds, and have nothing more to attain – still I adhere to *dharma*. 23 For were I ever to avoid tirelessly doing so, all mankind would follow my path. 24 Had I ceased adhering to my duties, all these worlds would have perished, and I would have caused miscegenation among the classes, as well as destroyed the hosts of creatures. 25 Just as the unwise perform their duties out of interest, the wise do so disinterestedly, desiring the welfare of the world. 26 The wise one should not unsettle the ignorant whose minds are attached to different activities, rather he should encourage them to perform their duties and thus enjoy all sorts of action, while he himself acts in a controlled manner.

Commentary

A revolutionary statement is made: following *dharma* is not mandatory under any circumstance; if one has achieved the position of satisfaction in the self, or, in other words, is situated in the 'second tier', he is exempt from the injunctions of *dharma*. The seeds of this idea are to be found earlier in the second chapter, where Kṛṣṇa, having rejected Arjuna's arguments in favour of adherence to *dharma*, has offered a change of grounds by proposing the second-tier worldview as an alternative to the first.[14] A possible counter-argument on Arjuna's side could have been: 'if so, let us occupy ourselves with enlightenment, and abandon the battle'. However, this argument has already been dealt with in the opening section of this chapter and, as such, a different direction is to be sought. The question now is how does Kṛṣṇa justify fighting according to *dharma*, having claimed that the enlightened is exempt from it. Of course, it has not been expressly stated that Arjuna has achieved enlightenment, but this possibility seems to be taken into account. Kṛṣṇa now analyses the situation of the enlightened established in the self; on the one hand he has no need, duty or motive to act in this world, while on the other hand he has no

[14] *BG* 2.11–15.

need, motive or cause to avoid performing his *dharmic* duty. How, then, should he conduct himself? In this regards, Kṛṣṇa mentions King Janaka and others who had attained perfection through adherence to duty, and thereby underscores that by adhering to *dharma* one can attain success. As Kṛṣṇa asserts that the general public follows the example of great men, the conclusion is inevitable: perform your *dharmic* duty in order to set an example for the public to follow. Kṛṣṇa then mentions himself as an example of one not obliged to perform any *dharmic* duties, but who nevertheless acts in this manner in order to set an example for the general public. This statement is somewhat surprising, considering that Arjuna hears it from his charioteer, cousin and friend, who so far has not claimed any superhuman identity. This issue will be soon settled when Arjuna will ask Kṛṣṇa directly as to his identity,[15] and when Kṛṣṇa will state that he is the supreme descending to earth.[16] At any rate, Kṛṣṇa pursues his arguments, saying that if Arjuna does not adhere to his *dharmic* duty and does not fight, the hosts of creatures will be lost because of the harm caused to *dharma*, and the miscegenation among the social classes which will ensue. In saying this, Kṛṣṇa reverses Arjuna's arguments: Arjuna has previously stated that if he fights *dharma* will be harmed, the world order will be impaired and a miscegenation among classes will ensue;[17] Kṛṣṇa now replies that all this will happen if Arjuna declines to fight.

The *Guṇas* Alone are Acting – as such it is Best to Adhere to Duty

> 27 Although actions in every respect are performed by the *guṇas* of material nature, the spirit soul, confused by the ego thinks: 'It is actually me who is the doer'. 28 But he who knows the truth, O mighty Arjuna, regarding the separation (of the soul) from both the *guṇas* and activity, and sees clearly that the *guṇas* act among themselves – he is not attached. 29 Those thus bewildered by the *guṇas* of material nature, are attached to actions within the *guṇas*' scope. However, he whose knowledge is complete may not disturb those fools whose knowledge is incomplete. 30 Surrendering all your activities unto me with mind fixed on the highest self, without desire and avoiding possessiveness, cast lethargy aside and fight! 31 Those who always follow this doctrine of mine while being faithful and eschewing envy, they too are released from their *karma* bondage. 32 But those who reject my teachings out of envy and thus do not practice them, are deluded in all their knowledge; know that these fools are lost. 33 Even a learned man acts according to his own nature, as all beings follow their nature; therefore, what can repression accomplish? 34 Attraction and repulsion between the senses and their objects certainly exist, but one should not fall under their power, as both are foes. 35 Better to be deficient in following one's own *dharmic* duty, than to

[15] *BG* 4.4.
[16] *BG* 4.6–8.
[17] *BG* 1.40–44.

perform another's duty well; even death while performing one's own duty is better, for following another's duty invites danger.

Commentary

Whereas the ignorant believe that they act independently despite their being conditioned and bound by the *guṇas*, the learned are aware of the *guṇas*' total control over them. The question may be raised: are the learned who are aware of the *guṇas*' control free from their bonds? This is denied as the learned are forced to act according to their nature, just as all other beings do. It is therefore futile to suppress one's tendencies springing from one's nature, rather these should be met through adhering to one's natural *dharmic* duty. Still, the learned act without being attached to the fruits of their work, and their activity is aimed at giving an example to the general populace, in contrast to the ignorant who act out of a desire for the fruits of their work, and who are therefore impelled to act by the impulses of the *guṇas* alone. Shifting to a more personal tone, Kṛṣṇa asks Arjuna to fight for his sake, fix his mind on the self, and become free from passion and egotism; this is a call for personal devotion accompanied by a *yogic* state of mind. As such, an identity is formed between the stage of being fixed in the self, a stage where one is exempt from the *dharmic* duty, and the stage of direct service to Kṛṣṇa himself. Kṛṣṇa expands this into a universal philosophy and says that those who always follow this idea of his, in faith and without jealousy, are released from the bondage of action and reaction; conversely, those who reject his instructions out of jealousy are lost. A further interesting position is Kṛṣṇa's address to Arjuna, phrased as an imperative, avoiding rationalization: 'fight for me'. Possibly this is a position which will only lose from adding any further explanation. Perhaps Kṛṣṇa offers Arjuna devotion unsupported by logic as a position suggested to one who is exempt from *dharmic* duties; only later, possibly following Arjuna's hesitation, he supplies some argumentation, by saying that in this way Arjuna will be delivered from bondage. It is therefore to be noted that the fourth step in the ethical ladder, the step of activity for the sake of attaining *Brahman*, can also be defined as a service to Kṛṣṇa himself in a *yogic* frame of mind. The section ends with an unequivocal declaration which summarizes the topic of adherence to *dharma*: it is better to follow one's own *dharmic* duty even imperfectly, than to perfectly follow another's *dharmic* duty. By now, nearing the end of the third chapter the direction Kṛṣṇa pursues is gradually becoming clear; Arjuna should externally adhere to his warrior *dharma* while internally pursue the spiritual path and set *mokṣa* as his goal.

The Real Enemy is Lust

36 Arjuna said: What is it that impels one to commit evil, even against his will, as
if driven by force, O descendent of Vṛṣṇi? 37 The blessed Lord said: It is lust, it

is anger, originating from the passion-*guṇa*, and it is the great evil and the great
devourer; know that to be the enemy. 38 As fire is obscured by smoke, as a mirror
is covered by dust, and as the embryo is enveloped in the womb, so the living
being is obscured by lust.[18] 39 This eternal enemy covers even the wise one's
knowledge, O Kaunteya, having taken the form of this insatiable fire – lust. 40
It is said to abide in the senses, the mind and the intelligence; through these it
deludes the embodied soul and clouds its knowledge. 41 Therefore Bull among
the Bharatas, you should control the senses first; then destroy this evil, the
destroyer of knowledge and insight. 42 It is said that the senses are elevated, but
above the senses is the mind. The intelligence is still higher than the mind, but
superior even to the intelligence is the soul. 43 O mighty armed Arjuna, knowing
yourself as higher than the intelligence, let the self steady your mind and destroy
the indomitable enemy that takes the form of lust.

Commentary

Arjuna enquires as to the force which drives one to perform evil action, even against one's will or interest; Kṛṣṇa replies that it is lust which is situated in the senses, the mind and the intelligence. It overshadows the soul's true knowledge, it burns like an insatiable fire and it impels one to perform evil action; lust is the foe within and it is to be curbed through sense restraint. The underlying reasoning appears to be: 'the real enemy is within and that is lust; defeat it by controlling your senses, and in order to do so, you have to exercise *karma yoga*, or perform your *dharmic* duty as a *yoga* practice, i.e. externally fighting while internally seeking enlightenment. The external fighting will also contribute to your internal fighting by which you will vanquish the real enemy within – lust.' This argument sums up the chapter by pointing at the relation between action according to *dharmic* duty, and internal *yogic* action which aims at spiritual emancipation or *mokṣa*.

[18] *Idam*, 'this' can be taken as 'this world' too; as such, instead of the living being obscured by lust it would be the world which is obscured by lust.

Chapter 4
The Supreme Person's Descent

Kṛṣṇa is the Supreme Person Appearing in this World to Uplift *Dharma*

1 The Blessed Lord said: I propounded this imperishable *yoga* to Vivasvat, the
sun god; Vivasvat in turn imparted it to Manu, the father of mankind, and Manu
instructed Ikṣvāku in it. 2 In this way, this knowledge was transmitted through a
traditional succession of disciples and as such it has become known to the wise
kings; however, over a long period on earth, this *yoga* has been lost, O Parantapa.
3 I now impart this selfsame ancient *yoga* to you, for you are my devotee as well
as my friend; indeed, this is the ultimate mystery. 4 Arjuna said: as your birth
was later, whereas Vivasvat's birth was earlier; how can I comprehend that you
taught him this wisdom in the distant past? 5 The Blessed Lord said: many births
have I passed, and so did you, O Arjuna; I know all of them, but you know
not, O Parantapa. 6 Although I was never born and I myself am imperishable,
and although I am the Lord of all beings, when I take on material nature that I
own and control, I come into being through my own supernal power. 7 Indeed
whenever a decline in *dharma* occurs, and a surge of *adharma* – then I myself
appear. 8 To rescue the good and the pious, to destroy evil doers, and to re-
establish *dharma*, I myself descend age after age. 9 He who thus knows in truth
of my divine birth and deeds, after leaving his body is not brought to birth again,
rather to me he goes, O Arjuna. 10 Freed from desire, fear and anger, absorbed in
me and seeking refuge in me, many became purified through the fire of wisdom,
and have thus attained my nature. 11 As they surrender unto me, I reward them
accordingly. In any case, men follow my path in all respects, O Pārtha.

Commentary

The chapter begins with Kṛṣṇa delineating the history of the knowledge he is propounding; accordingly, he had passed this knowledge of *yoga* to humanity in the distant past, and now he passes this very same knowledge to Arjuna. The latter's qualification for receiving this knowledge is his close relationship with Kṛṣṇa, since Arjuna is his devoted follower and concurrently his friend. Since Kṛṣṇa is Arjuna's cousin and is of a similar age, the question is naturally raised, how is it possible for Kṛṣṇa to have passed this knowledge to the sun god in the remote past, apparently some millions of years ago? Kṛṣṇa answers that they have both undergone many births in the past, births which he himself remembers while Arjuna does not. At this point, Kṛṣṇa dramatically reveals his divinity, and declares his position as the Supreme Ruler of all, possessing supernatural powers.

Kṛṣṇa now propounds the famous *avatāra* theme: wherever *dharma* is weakened or harmed, and *adharma* is on the rise – there and then he himself appears; the purpose of his appearance is the re-establishment of *dharma*, the protection of the pious and the destruction of the evil-doers. Next Kṛṣṇa returns to address the theme of knowledge, which constitutes the chapter's main theme; he declares that he who knows the nature of his birth and deeds attains liberation; apparently, many in the past who were in possession of this knowledge, were purified by the fire of this wisdom,[1] and were thus fortunate to reach Kṛṣṇa. At last, Kṛṣṇa defines the basic relationship between himself and the created beings, namely reciprocity; as one relates to the supreme, so does the supreme relate to him. This section offers a 'second tier' worldview; from this viewpoint Arjuna sees the living beings bound in repeated cycles of birth and death, along with the perpetual conflict and struggle between *dharma* and *adharma*, and he sees the Supreme Person intervening in history, aiming at strengthening the pious and liberating the devotees. At last, the ideal of personal devotion as a means for liberation is articulated; hence the text proceeds to discuss the nature of activity.

The Doctrine of Action: Acting without Bondage

> 12 Those desiring success through *Vedic* rituals, sacrifice to the gods here in this world, for success born of such rituals comes quickly indeed in the world of men. 13 I have created the four social classes according to the divisions of the *guṇas* and modes of work; although I am the creator of this system, know that I am forever a non-doer. 14 Actions taint me not, as I have no desire for their fruits; nor is he who understands me as such bound by actions. 15 As they knew this and desired liberation, even the ancients resorted to action; therefore, you too should act as the ancients did in the past. 16 What is action? What is inaction? Even the wise are confused in this matter. Now I shall explain this matter of action to you; having understood this you shall be free from evil. 17 One must know what action (*karma*) is, one must know what improper action (*vikarma*) is, and one must know what inaction (*akarma*) is, as profound indeed is the course of action. 18 He who sees non-action in action, and action in non-action is held enlightened among men; despite performing all sorts of actions, he is yoked.[2] 19 He whose enterprises are all devoid of intent to satisfy lust, and whose *karma* has been burnt in the fire of knowledge, is called wise by the enlightened sages. 20 Having relinquished attachment to the fruits of action, ever satisfied and self-sufficient, although engaged in activity in fact he does nothing at all. 21 Free from desire and his mind controlled, having relinquished all sense of possessiveness and acting only for the body's bare necessities, even if engaged in activity no evil reaction touches him. 22 He who is satisfied with gain that comes of itself, who

[1] Or 'the austerity of knowledge'.

[2] Yoked – *yuktaḥ*.

transcends the dualities, who is devoid of envy and who accepts alike success and failure – is not bound even when he acts.

Commentary

This section further develops the theme of disinterested action;[3] for this purpose it first looks into the nature of the *Vedic* ritualistic sacrifices performed with the aim of achieving worldly success and prosperity.[4] The implicit critique is that these sacrifices are performed for mere worldly gains as opposed to liberation. As the *Vedic* sacrifices are performed within the *dharmic* social structure called *varṇāśrama*, an objection may be raised; what is wrong in performing these *Vedic* sacrifices, by whose performance *dharma* is being properly adhered to? Kṛṣṇa answers by further developing the *Bhagavad Gītā*'s philosophy of action; by articulating the notion of '*karma*-free' action which is considered to be 'inaction', he points at the recommended mode of adhering to *dharma* as opposed to the performance of *dharma* for the purpose of worldly success. Kṛṣṇa first looks into the *Vedic* social structure, and says that one's position within that structure is determined by *guṇa* and *karma*, as the spirit soul is conditioned by a certain mixture of the *guṇas*, and that determines one's tendency of work. Accordingly those conditioned by the higher *guṇas* are the *brahmins*, those whose nature is constituted of a somewhat lower mixture of the *guṇas* are the *kṣatriyas*, those whose nature is constituted of a lower mixture of *guṇas* are the *vaiśyas*, and those conditioned by a still lower mixture of the *guṇas* are the *śūdras*. In saying that, Kṛṣṇa raises the discussion to the 'second tier', where the human being is seen as a spirit soul conditioned by the *guṇas*. Kṛṣṇa now explains the manner in which he acts; although he acts, he himself is a non-doer. The reason is that he has no desire for the fruits of actions, and therefore is not tainted by *karma* or reactions; this is the ideal to be followed by Arjuna – the ideal of untainted or pure action. If Arjuna could see himself as a spirit soul conditioned by a certain mixture of the *guṇas* leading him to act as a warrior, and if he could act in this capacity for the purpose of liberation – he could then act purely and be considered a non-doer even while fighting. Three concepts are defined: proper activity[5], improper activity[6] and inactivity.[7] Activity is performed according to *dharma*, and breeds good results such as worldly success and the attainment of heaven. Ritualistic activity belongs to this category, and hence the inherent flaw; it produces *karma*, whereas improper activity is activity opposed to *dharma*, and includes immoral deeds or sins. Such activity results in various kinds of suffering, such as rebirth in lower planets, in animal or plant forms; it is this kind of activity which Arjuna considers the fighting

---

3 *BG* 2.47.

4 *BG* 2.42–43.

5 *Karma*.

6 *Vikarma*.

7 *Akarma*.

to be.[8] Activity of the third kind is the most interesting and this is the ideal to be followed: it is inactivity, and accordingly disinterested action is considered inaction in that it is free from *karma*. How can Arjuna's suggestion to relinquish fighting altogether[9] now be categorized? It could be taken either as proper action or improper action, but certainly not as inaction.

Sacrifice as Means for Attaining the Supreme

> 23 The reactions following activity (*karma*) dissolve for him who performs sacrifice, who is liberated and freed from attachment, and his mind given over to knowledge. 24 *Brahman* is the offering and *Brahman* is the oblation, that is poured into the fire of *Brahman* by *Brahman*; he who thus contemplates the act of sacrifice, attains *Brahman*. 25 Some *yogīs* worship the gods alone through sacrifice, while others sacrifice through offering in the fire of *Brahman*. 26 Still others sacrifice the senses such as hearing in the fire of self-restraint, while some offer the objects of the senses such as sound, in the fire of the senses. 27 Others offer all the actions of the senses and the movements of the life air in the fire of self-control *yoga*, a fire which is kindled by the torch of knowledge.[10] 28 Stringently self-controlled and following strict vows, some sacrifice material possessions, some sacrifice through austere practices, some through the performance of *yoga*, whereas others sacrifice through study and recitation of the *Veda*. 29 Some offer the inhalation into the exhalation, and the exhalation into the inhalation; thus restraining the process of breathing they are intent on controlling the life air. 30 Others thus restricting their food offer the life air into itself; all these know the meaning of sacrifice and all their sins are destroyed by it. 31 Having eaten the nectar of the sacrifice's remnants, they go to the eternal *Brahman*. O best of the Kurus, not even this world is for him who does not sacrifice; how then the next? 32 Thus diverse sorts of sacrifices spread out in *Brahman's* mouth; know them all to be born of action, as by knowing them thus, you shall attain liberation. 33 The sacrifice of knowledge is superior to the offering of material possessions, O Parantapa, as the peak of all activities, without exception, is the attainment of knowledge.

Commentary

The idea of inaction is not merely theoretical, rather it is applied and practiced through sacrificial activity. When the sacrifice is accompanied by true knowledge of the ultimate purpose behind the sacrifice, i.e. the attainment of *Brahman*, and when it is performed out of an inner state of non-attachment, the sacrificial

---

8 *BG* 1.36–39.

9 *BG* 1.46.

10 The 'Torch of knowledge': literally 'kindled by knowledge'.

activity becomes inaction. In order to exemplify this, various sorts of sacrifices are presented; some are *Vedic* such as worship of the gods or sacrifice of material possessions, whereas some are *yogic*, such as sacrifice through breath control and sacrificing the objects of the senses in the fire of the senses. However, the role of true knowledge in the sacrifice is essential; not only does the torch of knowledge light the fire of sacrifice, or endow it with a deeper meaning, but the sacrifice of knowledge is taken to be the highest form of sacrifice. The sacrifice may also metaphorically represent the forthcoming battle; accordingly, the battleground may be perceived as a huge sacrificial arena, and fighting the war as a sacrificial activity.[11]

Knowledge and its Fruit

> 34 Know this by falling at the feet of the master, asking him questions and offering him service; in so doing, men of wisdom and vision of the truth will impart knowledge unto you. 35 Endowed with this knowledge you will not fall again into delusion, O son of Pāṇḍu, and shall see all living beings in the self, and also within me. 36 Even if you are the worst sinner of all villains you shall cross over all evil just by ascending the boat of knowledge. 37 O Arjuna, as fire reduces wood to ashes, so the fire of knowledge burns all one's *karma* to ashes. 38 For in this world there is no purifier equal to knowledge; one who has attained the perfection of *yoga*, in time realizes this within himself. 39 The faithful who aspires for it and who has mastered his senses attains this knowledge, and thence he soon attains deep serenity. 40 However, he who is without faith, ignorant and riddled with doubt perishes; in fact, he who is full of doubts achieves not this world, nor the next, nor even happiness. 41 O Dhanañjaya, He who has renounced activity through *yoga*, whose doubts have been severed by knowledge and is self-possessed, is not bound by actions. 42 Therefore, O Bhārata, you should cut the doubt that springs from naught but ignorance out of your heart, and with your own sword of knowledge, resort to *yoga* and arise to battle!

Commentary

This metaphor-laden section summarizes the chapter while it returns to the opening theme, namely knowledge and the process of its reception. Knowledge is obtained from the *guru* who represents the unbroken succession of teachers

[11] For this metaphor see *Mahābhārata*, 5.139.29–55: Accordingly, Kṛṣṇa will witness the great sacrifice of war, and will accept the role of the *adhvaryu* brahmin; Arjuna will accept the role of the *hotṛ* and his weapons will be the mantras performing the sacrifice. Bhīma will accept the role of *udgātṛ* and Yudhiṣṭhira the role of the *brāhmaṇa*; the spears and clubs will serve as sticks lighting the sacrificial fire and the spilled blood will comprise the offering.

called *paramparā*; in order to acquire such knowledge, the student must prostrate himself at the feet of his master, ask him questions and provide him with personal services. The teacher possesses not only theoretical knowledge but also direct experience, vision or *darśana*. Knowledge liberates one not only from illusion, but also from evil, since it burns the reaction to one's deeds or *karma*, and this is illustrated by two metaphors; the ship and the bonfire. In order to gain such knowledge, one must be steeped with faith, as the doubting one will not attain such knowledge, he will not be successful in this world or in the next. One who is able to overcome his doubts through this knowledge becomes free from bondage and *karma*. The chapter thus ends with the instruction that Arjuna must wield the sword of knowledge, rid himself of his doubts and get up and fight. First, the inner combat against doubt and ignorance must be fought, and after winning that internal battle, the external battle is to be contested.

Chapter 5

The Path of Enlightened Action – Part II

The Path of Knowledge and the Path of Action Both Lead to Liberation, but Action is Preferable

1 Arjuna said: O Kṛṣṇa, while exhorting me to relinquish action, you praise the
path of *yogic* action; please make entirely clear to me which one of the two is
preferable? 2 The Blessed Lord said: Both relinquishing activity and *yogic* action
lead to the highest good, but of the two, *karma yoga* or *yogic* action exceeds
renouncing action altogether. 3 He who neither hates nor desires is to be known
as always in the state of renunciation; indifferent to the pairs of dualities, he is
easily liberated from bondage, O mighty armed Arjuna. 4 Not the learned but
rather fools are those who claim *Sāṅkhya* and *yoga* to be different and separated,
as each when properly undertaken yields the fruit of both. 5 Those who practice
yoga can also reach the position attained by the practitioners of *Sāṅkhya*; he who
sees that *Sāṅkhya* and *yoga* are one and the same actually sees. 6 Difficult is it
indeed to attain renunciation which is not supported by the practice of *yoga*, but
the wise one absorbed in *yoga* quickly attains *Brahman*.

Commentary

Should action be relinquished or practiced? This core question which comprises the *Bhagavad Gītā*'s central dilemma was already raised and discussed,[1] but due to its importance it opens this chapter, this time in a slightly different emphasis. The given answer is that while the two paths, that of action and that of relinquishment, both lead to the supreme good, the course of *yogic* action is preferred over the theoretical path, which rejects action in favour of renunciation and the development of theoretical knowledge. The reason for this is that renunciation is difficult to achieve without the support of *yoga*; this is so because the mere rejection of worldly life out of aversion and out of consideration of its illusory nature leads one to the negative contemplation of the world. In other words, the maintenance of a detached spirit may require an attitude of aversion or repulsion which keeps one's mind absorbed in the world and hinders the development of indifference; as such, only a superficial renunciation is achieved in this way. Conversely, one who has attained the stage of inner bliss, or an actual and positive *yogic* experience, can in fact detach himself from the world, as the external world of sensual objects cannot compare to the richer inner world achieved by him. The section is summarized

---

[1] *BG* 3.1–8.

by stating that it is difficult to attain renunciation which is not supported by *yoga* practice; this topic requires a further clarification, and it indeed becomes the central theme of this chapter.

External Detachment and Internal Bliss

> 7 He who is absorbed in *yoga*, who is a pure soul, who is self-controlled and has subdued his senses, and who is deeply related to all living beings, is never defiled even though he acts.[2] 8–9 'I am not really doing anything', reflects the knower of the truth absorbed in *yoga*. While seeing, hearing, touching, smelling, eating, walking, sleeping, breathing, evacuating, receiving, opening or closing his eyes, he meditates and considers all these as nothing but the senses acting among their sense objects. 10 He who acts without attachment, offering his actions to *Brahman*, is not tainted by evil, as the lotus leaf is not made by water. 11 Having cast aside their attachments, the *yogīs* act with their mind, intelligence, body and even with their senses for the purpose of self-purification. 12 Having given up the fruits of his actions, he who is absorbed in *yoga* attains deep and lasting peace. However, he who does not maintain this state of mind, who is attached to those fruits and acts out of lust for them, is fettered. 13 When the soul residing in the body renounces all actions mentally, it resides happily and rules the nine-gated city (the body) neither acting nor accumulating *karma*.

Commentary

The ideal agent is not defiled by his deeds, as his mode of action is *yogic*, i.e. it is *karma yoga* or '*yoga* of action'; the section looks into the inner attitude of this master of activity, whose position is summarized by the statement 'I am actually not doing anything'. While dwelling in the body, he observes his senses engaged with their objects, as if he was observing an external phenomenon. As such, he sees that the senses are driven by the sense objects, or seen from a wider perspective, by the *guṇas*. The tenth verse takes this idea a step further; it not only describes how action is external to oneself, rather it also offers a way of acting without being tainted by activity, and that – through dedicating one's deeds to *Brahman*. The notion of *Brahman* will soon develop into a concrete and personalized notion, with the call for dedicating sacrifices and austerities unto the Supreme Person.[3] The aim

---

[2] The phrase *sarva bhūtātma bhūtātmā* invites various interpretations. Śaṅkara takes it as supporting the *advaita* doctrine, in that a specific soul has become one with all souls. Rāmānuja's interpretation is that 'he finds that his self is similar to the self of all beings'. I translate it is as 'deeply related to all beings' thus accepting various possible relations between oneself and all beings: oneness, similarity and considering all beings dear to oneself.

[3] *BG* 5.29.

of the *yogī* described in this section is inner purification; in order to achieve this he utilizes his body, soul, intelligence and even the most dangerous of all – the senses. His efforts permit him to achieve an inner state of deep peace and bliss; this inner pleasure of the *yogī*, whose aim is purification, explains how external renunciation should be supported by *yoga*, or by a constant internal effort towards purification. As such, while renunciation alone requires a state of mind of constant aversion to the world, the renunciation which is supported by *yoga* is characterized by a state of satisfaction and inner bliss. This inner state enables the *yogī* to continue acting in the world while maintaining an inner *yogic* state of detachment and bliss.

Who is Nevertheless the Doer of Action?

> 14 The lord of the body (the soul) is not the cause of action, neither of the relation of action to its fruits; these are all set in motion by his own nature. 15 Nor does the Supreme accept responsibility for anyone's wrong doings neither for their good deeds; it is ignorance which covers knowledge and causes living beings to fall into delusion. 16 But for those whose ignorance concerning the self is destroyed by knowledge, that knowledge which is bright as the sun, illuminates the Supreme. 17 Those whose consciousness, self, determination and devotion are all directed towards the Supreme, go never to return again, as knowledge has cleansed their faults away. 18 Wise indeed are they who see no difference between a learned brahmin of distinguished bearing, a cow, an elephant, a dog and even an outcaste dog-eater.

Commentary

After learning that the soul dwelling in the body is not the cause of action represented by the interrelation of the senses and their objects,[4] the question arises: who nevertheless performs the action and is held responsible for it? It appears that three answers are possible; the soul, nature and the supreme. In order to elucidate this idea an example may be offered; a thief is caught in the act by the police, and is sentenced and sent to jail. The question may arise, who is responsible for his imprisonment? Three possible answers may be offered:

1. He alone brought the punishment upon himself (the soul).
2. The police who caught him, handcuffed him and locked him behind bars (nature).
3. The judge who sentenced him to be jailed (the supreme).

It seems that all three answers could be accepted as true, and each could be emphasized at times. The present discussion is concerned with *karma yoga*, which

---

[4] *BG* 5.8–9.

represents a state of action intertwining an inner *yogic* state of mind with an external action. As the realization of embodiment implies a sense of being helpless under the regime of the *guṇas*, the text here points at nature, which is consisted of the *guṇas*, as responsible for external action. This leaves the *yogī* responsible for internal activity, i.e. striving for purification and liberation, while on the opposite side, ignorance, which covers one with illusion, can be blamed for the absence of internal activity. Verses 14 and 15 may be read now in light of this view; first, it is stated that it is not the soul which induces activity, rather it is human nature.[5] Next it is asserted that the supreme is not responsible for one's good or bad deeds, and finally it is said that ignorance is the cause of illusion. The conclusion is that it is human nature which in fact is responsible for the action and its effect or *karmic* reaction; this answer is indeed suitable for the level of *karma yoga*, the level with which the chapter deals. Following this discussion, the text proceeds to point at the remedy for ignorance, namely knowledge; it shines like the sun and illuminates the supreme. Moreover, those who have attained such knowledge see their goal clearly and advance towards it, until they achieve liberation from *saṁsāra*. Knowledge has a cleansing quality, an idea which was already encountered at the end of Chapter 4.[6] Those possessing such knowledge gain an equal vision, and thus regard the brahmin and the dog-eater as equal; this is so as both of them are in fact souls encaged within bodies.

The Ideal *Yogī*

19 Those who have attained mental equanimity have conquered rebirth even while
living in this world; they are established in *Brahman*, as *Brahman* is indeed
faultless and impartial. 20 Such a person may not rejoice upon achieving the
desired, nor regret upon receiving the undesired. With a steady consciousness
and not deluded, he is a true knower of *Brahman*; as such he is established
in *Brahman*. 21 He is unattached to external sensual contacts, he finds within
himself great bliss, he is absorbed in *Brahman* through *yoga*, and as such he
relishes permanent happiness. 22 Those pleasures springing from sensual contacts
are indeed nothing but sources of misery; moreover, they have a beginning and
an end; as such the enlightened do not rejoice in them. 23 He who can withstand
the urges originating from lust and anger in this world, before release from the
body, is yoked and is a happy person. 24 He whose happiness is within, whose
pleasure is within, and his enlightenment too is within is actually a *yogī*; with his
whole being absorbed in *Brahman*, he attains to extinction in *Brahman*. 25 The
seers whose evils have been eradicated, who are free from doubt, self-controlled
and who wish all beings well, attain extinction in *Brahman*. 26 For those freed
from lust and anger, who are ascetics of controlled minds and who know the self

[5] Indicated by the word *svabhāva*.

[6] *BG* 4.37.

– for them close at hand lies extinction in *Brahman*. 27–28 Shutting out the sense impressions, focusing the gaze between the eyebrows, balancing inhalation and exhalation within the nostrils, restraining the senses, mind and intelligence – thus the sage who is intent on liberation and whose desires, fear and anger are gone – is indeed forever liberated. 29 Knowing me to be the enjoyer of sacrifices and austerities, as the great Lord of all the worlds, and as the friend who wishes well to all beings, he therefore attains deep peace.

Commentary

The chapter concludes with the description of the ideal *yogī*; on the one hand he rejects external sensual experiences, while on the other hand he cultivates inner bliss. This elucidates the statement made at the beginning of the chapter, declaring that it is difficult to attain renunciation unless it is supported by the practice of *yoga*.[7] External happiness and internal happiness are contrasted; external happiness originates in ephemeral sensual experiences, and as such breeds only suffering, while internal happiness, attained through purification, self-restraint and immersion in *Brahman*, is eternal and never-ending. The expression '*brahma nirvāṇa*'[8] appears thrice; it is not necessarily a borrowed Buddhist expression, rather it possesses its own logic in the framework of the *Bhagavad Gītā*. The logic is that whoever has achieved eternal inner bliss does so concomitantly with the extinction of his earthly existence: no more *saṁsāra*, no more *karma* and no more control by the *guṇas*. Another concept mentioned here is the concept of the *yogī* already liberated in this body and in this world, also known as *jīvan mukta*; this suggests that one can live in the world and pursue his *dharmic* duties while maintaining an inward *yogic* consciousness. This discussion expands the fifth step in the ethical ladder of self-transcendence, a step of inner joy representing a gradual relinquishment of worldly attachments along with a gradual establishment in the spiritual reality. At last, the *yogic* condition called *pratyāhāra* or withdrawal is described;[9] having related withdrawal to *karma yoga*, the text will now proceed to discuss withdrawal from the point of view of *aṣṭāṅga yoga*, and this is the subject of the next chapter. In the concluding verse Kṛṣṇa points to himself as the supreme goal; the goal mentioned so far in a general, impersonal way as '*Brahman*' or '*Supreme*' will gradually develop into the Supreme in Person, and this direction will reach its peak in Chapters 7 and 9.

[7] *BG* 5.6.

[8] Extinction in *Brahman*.

[9] Verses 27–28.

Chapter 6
The Path of Classical *Yoga*

The Mind is a Friend and a Foe as Well

1 The blessed Lord said: He who performs his duty regardless of the fruits of
his actions, is indeed a renouncer and a *yogī*, and not he who doesn't light
the sacrificial fire nor avoids performing his duties. 2 That which is called
renunciation, know that to be the same as *yoga*, O Pāṇḍava, as indeed, no one
can become a *yogī* without first renouncing any selfish desire. 3 For the sage
desiring to ascend the *yoga* path, action is said to be the means, whereas for
him who has ascended and reached the height of *yoga*, extinction of external
activity is said to be the means. 4 When one loses interest in sense objects as well
as in activity, and gives up any external initiatives, it is said that the pinnacle
of *yoga* has been reached by him. 5 One should use his mind to raise himself,
and not to degrade himself, for the mind is indeed one's only friend – and one's
only enemy. 6 For one who has conquered the mind, this very mind will be his
friend, but for one who has failed to do so, his mind will be his bitter enemy. 7
For he who has conquered his mind and consequently attained a peace of mind,
the vision of the Supreme Person in the heart can be steadily maintained through
heat and cold, through happiness and distress and through honour and dishonour.
8 One who is absorbed in knowledge as well as in realization and is thus content,
fixed in contemplation and having conquered his senses – such a *yogī* is said to
be yoked indeed. With the same favour he looks upon a lump of clay, a rock,
and a piece of gold. 9 Yet more distinguished is one who regards equally friends,
allies, enemies, the neutral and the uninvolved parties, hateful men, kinsmen,
righteous and wicked.

Commentary

This chapter is engaged with the topic of classical *yoga*, which is a psychophysical system by which one refines his consciousness through different stages leading to the state of *samādhi* or enlightened introversion. It opens with a discussion contrasting activity and involvement in sacrificial ritualistic performances, with renunciation and the relinquishment of activity; this is the third discussion concerning this topic.[1] Here, too, *yoga* is recommended, but not *karma yoga* rather the eight-step *yoga* called *aṣṭāṅga yoga*, or a similar method; the third verse hints at this *yogic* transformational path by mentioning 'ascension', hinting at its

---

[1] The other two are *BG* 3.1–8 and 5.1–6.

resemblance to the climbing of a ladder. At the beginning of the *yoga* path, action is adhered to, whereas at the later and advanced stages action is relinquished;[2] accordingly, the lower steps of this ladder are active and more external, whereas the higher steps of this ladder are contemplative and more internal. The four lower steps – *yama*, *niyama*, *āsana* and *prāṇāyāma* – require active practice, through self-restraint, through injunctions to be followed, through the exercise of *yogic* postures and through exercising *yogic* breathing. Conversely, the higher steps – *pratyāhāra*, *dhāraṇā*, *dhyāna* and *samādhi* – require further introversion characterized by a cessation of active practice; as such, *pratyāhāra* requires detachment from the objects of the senses, *dhāraṇā* requires inner concentration, *dhyāna* involves meditation and the state of *samādhi* is entirely introverted. Following that the discussion turns to the mind and its control; as restraint and purification of the mind are at the heart of the *yogic* method, a great effort is invested by the practitioner to achieve that end. The unrestrained mind wanders and is attracted to the sense objects, thus binding the soul further and further in the world, removing it further from the path of liberation. Conversely, the restrained mind is engaged in meditation and purification, and as such liberates the soul from its worldly bonds. Therefore the mind may be considered both a friend and a foe, depending on whether it is restrained or not. The term *paramātman*[3] seems to suggest the *antaryāmin*, sometimes referred to as the second person dwelling in the heart, who is one of the objects of *yogic* meditation. At the end of the section the ideal of indifference and equanimity reappears, and whether purposely or not, indifference towards both enemies and allies is mentioned.

The Practice of *Yoga*

> 10 The *yogī* should be constantly absorbed in self-contemplation, in solitude and alone, self-controlled, without desire and without possessions. 11 He should establish himself a firm seat in a pure place, a seat neither too high nor too low, and should cover it with a cloth, a deer skin and *kuśa* grass. 12 There on that seat, he should focus his mind on one point, control his mental and sensual activities, and practice *yoga* for self-purification. 13 Holding his body, head and neck erect and motionless, fixing his gaze on the tip of his nose, not glancing aside, 14 in a state of deep serenity, his fear gone, fixed in celibacy, mind subdued, his consciousness fixed on me, he should sit absorbed and contemplate me as the Supreme. 15 In this way, as the *yogī* absorbs himself in *yoga* with a controlled mind, he achieves peace, complete extinction and union with me.

---

2 *BG* 6.3.

3 6.7.

Commentary

A brief exposition of the *yoga* system is offered; the description includes terms familiar from the *yogasūtra*, such as *āsana*,[4] *sthira*,[5] *ekāgra*[6] and *citta*.[7] When read carefully, it becomes apparent that this condensed section delineates the entire *yoga* system from the first step, *yama*, up to the eighth step of *samādhi*.[8] As such, the term *yata cittātmā*[9] is mentioned; it refers to restraining the self or the mind, and denotes a meaning similar to the famous *yogasūtra* aphorism *yogaś citta vṛtti niroddha*,[10] translated as '*yoga* is the restraint of mental fluctuations'. The term *aparigraha*[11] refers to the fifth stage of *yama* meaning non-possessiveness,[12] and the term *śaucam*[13] refers to the first stage of *niyama* and may be translated as purity or cleanliness.[14] The phrase *sthiram āsanam*[15] seems to be closely related to the phrase *sthira sukham āsanam* which may be translated as 'the posture should be steady and bring happiness',[16] and the term *tatraikāgraṁ manaḥ*[17] seems to refer to the mental state of *ekāgra*,[18] meaning 'single pointed mind'. Despite the apparent similarity to the *yoga-sūtra*, this section differs from it in its personal tone, expressed through the concentration on the Supreme Person as the main object of meditation; it seems that the *Bhagavad Gītā*'s version of *yoga* is more theistic, in that the Supreme Person is not only the object of meditation, but that union with him comprises the state of *samādhi*.

The Middle Way and the State of *Samādhi*

> 16 The path of *yoga* befits not him who eats too much, nor him who hardly eats, nor him who sleeps too much nor him who is ever awake. 17 For him who is moderate and restrained in eating, diversion, and activity, in sleeping and wakefulness, *yoga* dispels all misery. 18 When a man of restrained consciousness

4 Seat, posture.

5 Firm.

6 One pointed attention.

7 Mind, consciousness.

8 *Yogic* perfection, supreme internal awareness.

9 6.10.

10 *Yogasūtra* of Patañjali (henceforth *ys*), 1.2.

11 6.10.

12 See *ys* 2.30.

13 6.11.

14 See *ys* 2.32.

15 6.11.

16 2.46.

17 6.12.

18 See *ys* 2.41, 3.11–12.

is absorbed in the self alone, devoid of any hint of desire or lust, he is said to
be yoked indeed. 19 As the familiar saying goes, the candle flame in a windless
place does not flicker; so is it for the *yogī* of controlled mind absorbed and
focused on the *yoga* of the self. 20 When the consciousness rests peacefully,
restrained by practice of *yoga*, then can the self see itself directly, and be thus
satisfied within itself. 21 At that time he knows infinite bliss, experienced by an
internal consciousness beyond the senses; firmly established, he deviates not
from the truth. 22 Having attained this, he holds no other acquisition greater,
and thus situated, even grievous misery does not shake him. 23 Let it be known
that dissolution of the deep union with misery is called *yoga*, and it should be
practiced with whole-hearted determination.

Commentary

The 'middle way' or the moderate practice of *yoga* is called for; excessive enjoyment is not recommended nor is extreme asceticism. The reason is that both arouse a notion of self-consciousness, a mentality which hinders the *yogī* in his progress along the *yoga* path. This moderation which applies to the lower steps of the *yoga* ladder not only eases the suffering which is a natural outcome of embodied existence, but brings joy by raising one to the state of the *guṇa* of goodness. Following this cultivation of moderate practice, the stage of pacifying the consciousness through meditation and the condition of the self experiencing itself directly, subsequently attaining inner satisfaction, is described.[19] The peaceful consciousness is exemplified through a metaphor; the candle flame, stable in the absence of wind, exemplifies the *yogī*'s consciousness when fixed and free from mental fluctuations. At last, after the state of deep meditation, the peak of the *yoga* practice, i.e. *samādhi*, appears.[20] The *samādhi* experience entails not only happiness, but also a grasp of the truth in a non-intellectual and direct way, perceived without the disturbance generally caused by the fluctuations of the mind and senses. What is it that takes place in the *yogī*'s heart during the state of *samādhi*? It is undoubtedly hard to fathom the experience of the *yogī* in such an introspective and introverted state; still, one can surmise that possibly he encounters the *paramātman*[21] within himself, and this encounter yields a deep spiritual experience. It is also possible that he senses himself as spiritual, as also everything around him, similar to the vision described in the previous chapter.[22] Other experiences, such as experiencing oneness with *Brahman*, or various theistic devotional experiences are also conceivable. These experiences are so intense that one desires nothing more; moreover, nothing can disturb the mind of one who has attained this or attract him to return to the external world. The section ends with

19 6.19–20.

20 6.21–23.

21 *Antaryāmin*, the divine person within the heart.

22 *BG* 5.18.

the declaration that this constitutes the severance of the deep bond with suffering, or the world of *saṁsāra*, and therefore it must be practiced rigorously; this section undoubtedly offers one of the most exquisite and beautiful known descriptions depicting the state of *samādhi*.

The Worthwhile Struggle Against the Turbulent Mind

> 24 Casting aside all desires arising from worldly intentions, he should subdue
> completely the combined senses through the mind. 25 Little by little should he
> bring his mind to rest, while firmly controlling his consciousness; he should fix
> his mind on the self, contemplating nothing else. 26 From whatever and wherever
> the flickering and unsteady mind wanders, it is to be restrained and led back
> into the control of the self. 27 The *yogī* who has brought his mind to serenity
> indeed attains the highest bliss; his passions pacified, he becomes flawless and
> completely absorbed in *Brahman*. 28 The *yogī* who constantly practices this,
> becomes free from taint; easily he approaches *Brahman* and attains infinite
> happiness. 29 He who is deeply absorbed in *yoga* envisions the self as present in
> all beings, and envisions all beings as present in the self; as such he attains an
> equal vision under all circumstances. 30 For one who sees me everywhere, and
> sees everything in me, I am never lost, nor is he ever lost to me. 31 He who is
> absorbed in the vision of oneness, and under any circumstance worships me as
> present in all beings – he is a *yogī* indeed, and in me does he dwell. 32 O Arjuna,
> one who in relation to himself sees all beings equally, whether in happiness or
> distress, is considered the supreme *yogī*.

Commentary

The endeavour required from a *yogī* desiring to restrain the mind appears to be no less than a fierce battle. According to the *yogic* concept, the mind is perceived as a subtle organ which regulates the activity of the senses, and passes the impressions gathered by the senses to the intellect and thence to the soul. Emotions, thought and desire, are all within the function of the mind, and that in contrast to the intellect which analyses information and reaches consistent conclusions. The nature of the mind is stormy and capricious and its proximity to the senses fills it with incessant desires, with a continuous stream of thoughts, and with numerous different feelings culminating in attraction and repulsion. An unrestrained mind binds the soul continually to the world, in that it serves as a stimulant to worldly involvement. The systematic study of the mind and its various states is at the heart of the *yoga* system, and so is the major effort for its control. When the turbulent mind is curbed, restrained and subsequently becomes quiescent, it turns into a powerful aid for meditation; at this point it ceases to obstruct the *yogī*'s progress and is transformed from a foe to a friend. As the mind stops obstructing the experience of spirituality, various inner experiences which may well be considered mystical states appear, and some are herein described; the first is the blissful state which accompanies the experience of *Brahman*,[23] followed by a unifying experience of an impersonal nature, in which spiritual souls are seen everywhere.[24] In another vision the *yogī* sees the Supreme Person always and everywhere, and sees everything as resting in him;[25] this may well refer to the experience of the Supreme Person in the heart or *paramātman*, who is said to be present everywhere and to support everything. A personal touch is expressed through the warm relationships between the *yogī* and the Supreme Person; stated differently – the kind of *yoga* described here has a notable *bhakti* or devotional touch. At last, the *yogī* views all the various entities with equality and in comparison with himself.[26] As such, it seems that the various spiritual or *yogic* experiences are varied and personal, i.e. various *yogīs* may have different spiritual experiences and visions.

The Nature of the Mind and the Continuous Endeavour for Perfection

> 33 Arjuna said: O Madhusūdana, this system of *yoga* and equanimity you have just propounded, seems not founded on firm ground, because the mind is so capricious. 34 For the mind is restless, impetuous, mighty and unyielding, O Kṛṣṇa, I think restraining it would be as difficult as restraining the blowing wind. 35 The blessed Lord said: undoubtedly, O mighty armed, the mind is restless and difficult to curb; still, it can be controlled by constant practice and detachment. 36 Although I agree that this *yoga* system is difficult for one whose mind is uncontrolled, it is nevertheless possible for one who strives for such restraint by fitting means. 37 Arjuna said: What is the destination of one who follows this path faithfully, but without restraining himself? His mind thus deviates from the path of *yoga*, and so he does not attain to the state of perfection; where will he go? 38 O Kṛṣṇa, does he not fade away like a riven cloud, losing both worlds, having no solid ground, and straying from the path that leads to *Brahman*? 39 O Kṛṣṇa, please dissipate entirely this doubt of mine, as none can dispel it but you. 40 The Blessed Lord said: O Pārtha, not in this world nor in the next will he meet with destruction; O my friend, one who does good will never reach an evil destination. 41 Having attained the worlds of the righteous and dwelled therein for endless years, he who has deviated from the path of *yoga* is reborn in the home of pure and righteous people, or in a prosperous aristocratic family. 42 Or else, he is born into a clan of enlightened *yogīs*; undoubtedly, such a birth is rare in this world. 43 Hence he recovers the consciousness gained in his previous life, and from thence he strives again towards perfection. 44 The power of his previous practice attracts him to the path of *yoga*, sometimes even without his

[23] 6.28.
[24] 6.29.
[25] 6.30.
[26] 6.32.

wish, and he desires to know of it; as such he transcends the words of the *Vedas*.
45 Purified of all evils and attaining perfection by practicing restraint over many
births, he then goes to the supreme goal. 46 The *yogī* is superior to the ascetics,
the *yogī* is superior to the intellectuals and the *yogī* is superior to the performers
of rituals; therefore, O Arjuna, be a *yogī*! 47 And of all *yogīs*, he whose inner self
is absorbed in me, and who worships me with faith and love, him I deem to be
the best of all *yogīs*.

Commentary

Arjuna doubts the *yoga* system's practicality; since success is dependent upon curbing the mind, and since the mind is restrained only with great difficulty, the required mission seems impossible. Kṛṣṇa agrees that the task is difficult, but argues that with constant practice, accompanied by renunciation and detachment, the task may nevertheless be accomplished. Arjuna raises yet another question: what is the fate of one who tries to follow this course and renounces the world, but nevertheless turns out to be too weak to attain perfection; does he not lose both worlds? In his empathic reply Kṛṣṇa soothes Arjuna and declares that one who does good will never reach a an evil fate. As such, one who has exercised *yoga* and failed to achieve release from *saṁsāra* will live for many years in the heavenly worlds, and moreover, following this he will be reborn into a good family, perhaps even into a family of *yogīs*. At this time his dormant spiritual consciousness developed in the previous life will awaken, and he will continue his efforts towards liberation from the point at which he had stopped. Thus will he gain both worlds – this world through enjoying the heavenly worlds, and then the final liberation. The chapter's closing verse is no doubt one of the *Bhagavad Gītā*'s peaks: Kṛṣṇa urges Arjuna to accept the path of devotion as the devotional *yogī* is the topmost *yogī*. This also answers Arjuna's doubts; as a devotional *yogī*, he will immerse his mind in devotion to the Supreme Person, and this will restrain and pacify his mind; with his mind restrained in this way, he will no doubt attain success in the difficult path of *yoga*.

Chapter 7
The Vision of the Supreme – Part I

Introduction to the Highest Knowledge

1 The Blessed Lord said: O Pārtha, with your mind absorbed in me, being fixed in *yoga* and finding refuge in me, you can know me entirely and beyond doubt; hear now. 2 I shall now reveal to you fully knowledge accompanied by realization; having acquired this knowledge, nothing further in this world will remain to be known. 3 Among thousands of men, hardly anyone strives for perfection, and even among those who have striven and achieved perfection, hardly anyone knows me in truth.

Commentary

The central theological section of the *Bhagavad Gītā* now commences, and it continues up to the end of Chapter 12. In these six chapters,[1] Kṛṣṇa describes his divinity in detail and emphasizes the ideal of *bhakti* or devotion unto him. The opening statement consisting of three verses is significant and sets the agenda for the discussion about to start; Kṛṣṇa begins by defining the state of mind required of Arjuna, a state of mind which is a requirement for understanding the knowledge about to be revealed. The salient step taken in this brief section is the discussion's ascension from the second to the third tier; this level no longer propounds knowledge of sensual restraint, but knowledge of the Supreme Person and devotion unto him. The first characteristic of this new and higher state is *mayy āsakta manāḥ*, literally meaning 'with your mind absorbed in me'. The word *āsakta* is significant and means attachment; in his commentary on the first verse Zaehner refers to this and remarks:

> 'Attach your mind to me': this is utterly new and apparently at variance with the whole content of the last two chapters. There we had been told almost *ad nauseam* that we had to *detach* ourselves from everything: only by total detachment could liberation be won. Meditate on God certainly as a means of concentrating your mind, as the *Yoga-sūtras* recommend, but do not *attach* yourself to him or anything else because 'liberation' is clearly incompatible with attachment of any kind. Here, however, Arjuna is told most bluntly that this is not so: the true athlete of the spirit who has succeeded in integrating his personality and in becoming *Brahman* must now not only continue his spiritual

[1] With the reservation that Chapter 8 descends back to the second tier.

> exercise unremittingly, he must also attach his whole personality in all its new-found fullness and freedom to Kṛṣṇa who is God and, being God, transcends the immortal *Brahman* as much as he transcends the phenomenal world. Continued spiritual exercise preserving the integrated personality intact, attachment to God, and total trust in him are what Kṛṣṇa demands in this stanza.[2]

Zaehner points at the change occurring here: instead of practicing detachment from the world, as has been recommended so far, Arjuna is now encouraged to practice attachment to the Supreme Person. In other words, the phase of struggle with both attraction and repulsion towards sense objects ends with Chapter 6, and a new phase now begins, by which Arjuna is to view the world from a newer and higher point of view; accordingly, the world is no longer perceived as a threat, but as a manifestation of divine abundance. Kṛṣṇa emphasizes the significance of the knowledge he is about to disclose, and points out that perfection is attained by few, and even fewer are those who receive the knowledge of the supreme as a person.

Matter, the Spirit Souls and the Supreme Person

> 4 Earth, water, fire, air, ether, mind, intellect and ego – these eight comprise my separated lower nature. 5 But you should know that beside this lower nature, O mighty-armed one, there is another higher nature of mine, comprised of spirit souls, by which this world is sustained. 6 Realize that all entities have their source in these two natures.[3] I am the origin of this entire universe and of its dissolution too. 7 O Dhanañjaya, there exists nothing higher than me; everything rests upon me as pearls are strung on a thread. 8 I am the taste of water, O Kaunteya, and I am the light of the sun and the moon; I am the sacred syllable Oṁ in all the *Vedas*, the sound in ether, and the humanity in man. 9 The pure fragrance of the earth am I, and the brilliance in fire; I am the life of all living beings and the austerity of the ascetics. 10 Know me, Pārtha, to be the primeval seed of all creatures, the wisdom of the wise, and the splendour of the splendid. 11 And of the mighty, I am might devoid of lust and passion; that desire in all creatures am I, which is not inconsistent with *dharma*, O Bharatarṣabha. 12 Know that all states of being, be they characterized by *sattva*, *rajas* or *tamas*, have their source in me alone; but I am not in them – rather they are in me. 13 The entire world is deluded by the three states of being produced by the *guṇas*, and thus fails to recognize me, who am eternally above them.

---

[2] Robert Zaehner, *The Bhagavad-Gītā* (Oxford, 1969), p. 244.

[3] Although the text is not explicit in regards to the two natures, it is apparent that it refers to the two natures mentioned in verses 4–5. Both Śaṅkara and Rāmānuja refer to two natures; see also Franklin Edgerton, *The Bhagavad Gītā* (Cambridge, MA, 1972), note no. 2 to chapter 7, pp. 95–96.

Commentary

Kṛṣṇa now presents a theistic metaphysical dualism; the separate or lower nature makes up the gross and subtle aspects of the world, and the inseparate or higher nature is composed of spiritual souls which sustain the world, or cause its ongoing existence. As opposed to the *Sāṅkhya* dualism, the doctrine presented here is theistic; as such, both these natures rest upon the Supreme Person or comprise his nature, and he is the origin of everything, its maintainer and its ultimate dissolution. An analogy is given, according to which Kṛṣṇa is like the thread upon which the pearls are strung; although unseen, the thread comprises the foundation sustaining the pearls and holding them united. Kṛṣṇa offers various tangible examples which demonstrate the sense in which he is so close and underlies everything, such as the taste of water, the pure fragrance of the earth and the splendour of the splendid. A question may be raised, as to why is the supreme unseen if he is so close? The answer lies in the three *guṇas*, which act as a deluding veil; Kṛṣṇa himself is the *guṇas*' source and is eternally beyond them, but those who have not surrendered unto him cannot escape their tight control, and as such, fall under illusion and cannot see the supreme present everywhere.

It is Impossible to Overcome Illusion Unless One Surrenders to Kṛṣṇa

> 14 Divine indeed and difficult to penetrate is my deluding power, consisting of the three *guṇas*; but those who have surrendered unto me alone, they can transcend it. 15 Evil doers, deluded fools and vile men do not take refuge in me; thus, illusion deprives them of knowledge, and as such, they take their refuge in demonic existence. 16 Four kinds of pious men worship me, O Arjuna: the distressed, the seeker of knowledge, the seeker of wealth and the wise. 17 Highest among them is the wise, who is devoted to me alone and always absorbed in me, for I am very dear to him, and he is dear to me. 18 Noble indeed are all of them, but the wise I deem to be my very self, for he is firmly established as a soul absorbed in me alone, and I am his highest goal. 19 At the end of many births, the wise surrenders unto me, meditating that 'Vāsudeva is all in all'; difficult is it indeed to find such a great soul.

Commentary

Illusion is of a divine origin; it veils and hides the supreme from the embodied souls through the power of the three *guṇas*, and one cannot overcome it by himself. Moreover, it deprives the evil-doers from knowledge of the supreme, and directs them to take rebirth in lower demonic species. As opposed to the evil-doers, the pious take shelter in the supreme and surrender unto him. Although these pious people may still maintain some ulterior motives, such as approaching the supreme out of distress or out of a desire for wealth, they are all considered noble and apparently dear to Kṛṣṇa. The wise one, however, is especially dear because he has no other motive than knowing the Supreme Person. He gradually acquires more knowledge of the supreme, and becomes absorbed in meditation through which he sees Vāsudeva as all in all; this state frees him from further rebirth. The tone expressed by Kṛṣṇa is remarkably personal, as his devotees are indeed very dear to him. The point of view of the second tier, by which the souls were seen as bound in *saṁsāra*, and which promoted indifference and emotional restraint, is by now abandoned in favour of a higher level discourse, by which the reality of the Supreme Person is revealed. From this point of view one sees the supreme everywhere, and sees everything in relation to the supreme; this vision is accompanied by an intense emotional state, which is far different than the calm and transparent *yogic* state of mind. The good and the evil also take on different shapes; it is no more worldly success versus worldly failure, and no longer liberation versus bondage, as from the present point of view good and evil are defined in relation to the supreme. As such, the good are the pious devotees who worship the supreme, whereas the evil are the impious and demonic who do not take refuge in him. Let us examine the present discourse; from the ontological point of view, there exists a Supreme Person who possesses two natures – the lower nature represented by the phenomenal world comprised of eight gross and subtle material elements, and the higher nature comprised of spiritual souls. From the epistemological point of view, by taking refuge in the Supreme Person through devotion, one acquires knowledge, whereas by rejecting the Supreme Person, one is covered by illusion and is deprived of knowledge. From the ethical point of view, it is good to be devoted to the Supreme Person and worship him, while it is bad to reject him. The discourse has also ascended a step further along the 'ethical ladder'; it has progressed beyond the state of internal joy, and reached the state of proximity to the Supreme Person through devotion. Seen from this point of view, Arjuna should surrender unto Kṛṣṇa and, as an expression of devotion, follow Kṛṣṇa's will and fight the battle in a devotional state of mind.

Devotion to Other Gods Represents a State of Illusion

> 20 Those deprived of wisdom by various desires, resort to other gods. Although
> following various religious observances, they are nevertheless constrained by
> their own nature. 21 Whoever that devotee may be, and whatever divine form he
> may desire to worship faithfully, it is I who bestow that steady faith upon him.
> 22 Endowed with such faith, he endeavours to worship that deity and thus his
> desires obtain fulfillment; in fact by me alone are these desires fulfilled. 23 In any
> case, ephemeral is the fruit these people of little wit obtain; those who worship
> the gods will go to the gods, whereas my devotees will surely come to me. 24 The
> unintelligent consider me to be the non-manifest who has become manifest, not
> knowing my higher nature to be eternal and supreme. 25 Clouded by my illusory
> power I am not manifest to all, and thus the deluded world knows me not, who

am unborn and eternal. 26 O Arjuna, I know all creatures – those of the past, those
who now exist, and those who will come into being – but me no one knows. 27
From their birth, all living beings are covered by illusion with its surges of desire
and hate, due to the deluding power of the dualities. 28 But those of pious deeds,
whose evils have ended, are freed from that deluding power and worship me,
firm in their vows. 29 Having taken shelter in me, those striving for release from
old age and death know *Brahman* completely, as well as the self and activity. 30
Those knowing me as higher than the elements of creation, as the chief of gods,
and the principle of sacrifice, they, having their consciousness absorbed in *yoga*,
know me even in the hour of death.

Commentary

Kṛṣṇa's devotees are compared with devotees of other gods; as Kṛṣṇa has declared that his devotees rise above the illusion produced by the *guṇas*,[4] the question is raised, whether devotees of other deities rise above the *guṇas* too. Kṛṣṇa designates devotees of other gods as unintelligent and considers them to be motivated by worldly desires; he points out that despite following various religious observances and restraints, they are controlled by their own nature and, as such, are not able to rise above the *guṇas*. Kṛṣṇa then makes the surprising statement that he himself helps them acquire the faith needed for this sort of worship; moreover, it is him who grants them the fulfillment of their desires, although these desires are worldly and their fruits merely transient. Ultimately, the devotees of other gods will reach them, apparently in their next life, while Kṛṣṇa's devotees will reach him. Kṛṣṇa's sublime nature is hidden due to the illusion which veils the world; illusion covers everyone already from their birth, except those who are free from evil. It seems that being under illusion and being devoted to other gods are the characteristics of the evil-doers, whereas being free from illusion, free from worldly desires and being devoted to Kṛṣṇa are the characteristics of those who are free from evil. This appears to raise the discussion concerning evil to its climax, a discussion which has taken place especially during Chapters 2 and 3. Accordingly, complete deliverance from evil is possible in the state of unalloyed devotion to Kṛṣṇa, a state which can only be reached when freedom from the illusion of duality is attained, along with the freedom from the worldly desires accompanying such illusion.

---

4 *BG* 7.14.

Chapter 8

Quitting One's Body, the Ephemeral and Eternal Worlds

Arjuna's Eight Questions

1 Arjuna said: O Supreme Person, what is *Brahman*? What is the self? What is activity? What are the elements which constitute the creation? What is the divine? 2 What is the principle underlying sacrifice, and how does he reside in this body, O Madhusūdana? And how can the self-restrained know you at the hour of death? 3 The Blessed Lord said: The Supreme *Brahman* is the imperishable, and the self is said to be it's own nature; the creative force from which the nature of beings originates is known as action. 4 O best among the embodied, the elements that make up creation constitute but temporary existence; the divine is the Universal Person, and I, residing in the body, am the principle underlying sacrifice. 5 And he who at the end of his life, in his last hour, while leaving his body, remembers me alone – he will attain my being; of this there is no doubt.

Commentary

Chapter 7 ended with Kṛṣṇa's statement, that 'those knowing me as higher than the elements of creation, as the chief of gods, and the principle of sacrifice … know me even at the hour of death'.[1] It seems that this recollection or meditation on Kṛṣṇa at the hour of death, is the summit of a successful effort for liberation from rebirth; however, an explanation of the terms mentioned is required, and above that, an elaboration upon the topic of remembering the supreme at the time of departure is required, too. Arjuna's eight questions refer exactly to that: the first seven questions are concerned with the weighty terms mentioned at the end of Chapter 7; these are answered here by Kṛṣṇa in short, although they are elaborated upon elsewhere in the *Bhagavad Gītā*. Thus, *Brahman* is mentioned in many places throughout the text, what constitutes one's nature is described in Chapter 17,[2] a thorough discussion of activity appears in Chapters 3 and 4,[3] the elements are described in Chapters 7 and 13,[4] the universal form is described in Chapter 11

---

1 *BG* 7.30.

2 *BG* 17.3.

3 E.g. *BG* 3.21–24, 3.35, 4.16–18.

4 *BG* 7.4, 13.5–6.

and in a different way in Chapter 15,[5] and the principle of sacrifice is described in Chapters 3, 4 and 9.[6] All these are important questions and are broadly examined in the *Bhagavad Gītā* itself and in the *Upaniṣadic* literature as well. Following his brief replies which are reminiscent of the *sūtra* style, Kṛṣṇa answers the eighth and central question in detail; the question is 'how can the self-restrained know Kṛṣṇa at the hour of death', and henceforth the topic will serve as the central theme of the chapter. Having examined reality in the previous chapter from the third tier's point of view, this chapter's discourse goes back and examines the second tier's realm. However, as a higher point of view has by now been acquired, it now examines the struggle for liberation 'from above', so to speak. The chapter indeed displays this theme at its best, since it stresses on the one hand the bonds by which the embodied soul is fettered, and on the other hand the endeavour for liberation.

Remembering the Supreme Person while Leaving the Body Brings Release from the World

> 6 Every state of being remembered at the final moment, when one relinquishes his body – to that very state will he surely go, O Kaunteya, through transformation of his own being. 7 Therefore, at all times remember me and fight; with your mind and intelligence absorbed in me, you will come to me without doubt. 8 O Pārtha, he who meditates on the Supreme Divine Person through constant *yoga* practice, with an unswerving consciousness, goes to him. 9 One should meditate on him as the ancient seer, as the controller, as smaller than the atom, as the supporter of all, as having an inconceivable form, as brilliant as the sun, and beyond darkness. 10 His mind unwavering, absorbed in devotion, supported by the strength of *yoga*, his life air focused between the eyebrows – one who is thus established at the hour of death, reaches that Supreme Divine Person. 11 Now I shall explain to you briefly the path leading to the abode known by the sages of the *Veda* as the imperishable; ascetics desiring this abode practice celibacy and once freed from passion they enter it. 12 When all the body's gates are under control, when the mind is restrained in the heart, when the life air is held within the head, at that time one is established in *yogic* concentration. 13 He who leaves the body while pronouncing the single syllable which is *Brahman*, the Oṁ, while meditating on me, reaches the supreme goal. 14 O Partha, I am easily reached by the *yogī* who always remembers me, is constantly and fully absorbed in me, and is thus ever yoked. 15 Having come to me, these great souls do not again undergo rebirth into that transient abode of misery, as they have attained the highest perfection.

---

5 *BG* 11.9–12, 15.1–2.

6 *BG* 3.9, 4.12, 9.15–16.

Commentary

A fundamental principle is established; one's mental state at the hour of death determines one's next life. Accordingly, the soul quits the body enfolded by the subtle mental elements, which comprise one's empirical personality. The mental elements known also as the subtle body represent the state of one's consciousness; these crystallize during life and appear in a concentrated form at the moment of death. The subtle body is made of thoughts, convictions and mentality, attracts corresponding material elements which gather around it and form the next gross body. Thus one is born in a new body whose exterior conforms to the inner content it developed in its previous life. The new body is not necessarily human; it may be lower, such as a plant's or an animal's, and it may also be higher, such as a god's body. At any rate, be it a higher body or a lower one, the principle articulated here is that the new body is a natural outcome of the previous life's state of mind or consciousness.[7] The underlying logic here is that as Arjuna's goal is to be delivered from *saṁsāra*, he must remember Kṛṣṇa at the hour of departure from the body, and as this hour is unknown, Arjuna must always remember him. According to this idea,[8] Arjuna should fight and at the same time remember Kṛṣṇa; apparently, remembering Kṛṣṇa can be attained not only through a *yogic* type of meditation in solitude, but also through actively carrying out his order, such as by fighting. Accordingly, acting for Kṛṣṇa or under his instructions becomes a type of 'action-*yoga*' or *karma yoga*; this type of activity is of a *yogic* nature and has been discussed previously;[9] here, however, the emphasis lies on remembering Kṛṣṇa as an essential component of the *karma yoga* practice.

Having raised the subject matter of contemplation or meditation upon the supreme person, the text proceeds to elaborate on how this should be done, and what is the fruit of such meditation.[10] In this regards, the term *abhyāsa* is mentioned; it is a central concept in the *yoga* school describing repeated exercise, and it refers to the effort that must be invested in remembering the supreme. In order to facilitate this effort, various adjectives of the Supreme Person are given here. As mentioned before, Arjuna initially wished to avoid fighting by deserting the battlefield, and in this way indicated his wish to become a *yogī* and thus achieve perfection. Chapter 6 offered an in-depth discussion of *yoga*, and the present chapter develops the discussion further. As already mentioned, the point made is clear; the best way to practice *yoga* is by acting for Kṛṣṇa in the mood of devotion, while being conscious of him as the Supreme Person; in this way Arjuna will carry his duty of fighting, will become a *bhakti-yogī*, and will reach perfection. As the discussion focuses on the state of leaving the body, Kṛṣṇa describes the desirable way of doing so; this is done through *yoga* practice, through mastery of the life air and the contemplation

7 See also *BG* 15.7–11.

8 *BG* 8.7.

9 Such as in Chapter 3.

10 *BG* 8.8–10.

of the sacred *Oṁ*. However, the devoted need not practice this separately as for them, Kṛṣṇa will be easily attainable.

The Ephemeral World and the Eternal World

> 16 All the worlds, up to Brahmā's world, are subject to repeated births, but having once reached me, there is no further rebirth. 17 Those who know days and nights know Brahmā's day to last for a thousand ages, and his night to end after a thousand ages. 18 At the dawning of the day, all beings emerge from the unmanifest state to become manifest; at nightfall they dissolve, returning to their unmanifest state. 19 This multitude of entities comes into being again and again, only to dissolve helplessly with the fall of night, O Pārtha, and then originate again when day dawns. 20 Yet there also exists another state, unmanifest and eternal, which is higher than the former unmanifest state; while all beings perish, that state does not itself perish. 21 It is said to be eternal as well as imperishable, and they declare it to be the supreme destination; upon reaching it none returns here – that is my supreme abode. 22 That Supreme Person is attainable by single-minded devotion; within him all beings exist, and by him everything is pervaded.

Commentary

Kṛṣṇa now contrasts the material world with the spiritual world, apparently in order to further convince Arjuna that leaving this world and reaching the other world will be for his ultimate good. First, basic *purāṇic* cosmology is presented; accordingly, the universe is comprised of various constellations wherein the highest planet is that of Brahmā, the creator of the universe. The universe lasts for as long as Brahmā lives; when Brahmā is born the universe is created and, after a hundred years, at the time of his death the universe is dissolved. During Brahmā's life, partial cycles of universal creation and destruction take place, and these correspond to Brahmā's days and nights; when his night falls a partial ruin occurs, and when his dawn rises a partial creation takes place. The duration of an age or *kalpa* is a cycle of four *yugas*, altogether 4,320,000 years, and a duration of one thousand such *kalpas*, i.e. 4,320,000,000 years, makes one day of Brahmā; a similar duration comprises his night. For the duration of Brahmā's day, all beings become manifested, taking on bodies and acting under the *guṇas*; at his night, however, they enter an invisible state wherein the *guṇas* become inactive. As such, all beings helplessly resume activity during daybreak, to continue the struggle within *saṁsāra*, while at Brahmā's night they helplessly fall into a state of inactivity and sleep. As such, the situation of all beings is unfortunate, as they eternally struggle against nature through these enormous spans of time. As opposed to this state of existence, a different and ideal state is found; this is the state of living in the spiritual abode of the Supreme Person mentioned here only in brief.

Apparently, this state represents the highest goal to be aspired to and, referring to our model, it denotes the third tier in full.

Desirable and Undesirable Times for Leaving the Body

> 23 O best of the Bharatas, I shall speak now about the different times of departure,
> at which the *yogīs* return, or do not return. 24 Those *Brahman* knowing men who
> depart by fire, in the light, during the day, in the bright lunar fortnight and during
> the six months of the sun's northern course, go to *Brahman*. 25 However, those
> *yogīs* who depart in smoke, during the night, in the dark lunar fortnight and
> during the six months of the sun's southern course, thus obtaining the lunar light,
> attain rebirth. 26 These two universal paths, the light and the dark, are considered
> to be eternal. By the first – one does not return; by the other – he returns again.
> 27 Knowing these two paths, the *yogī* is not at all confused; therefore, at all times
> be absorbed in *yoga*, O Arjuna. 28 By knowing all this, the *yogī* transcends even
> the fruits of piety attained by studying the *Vedas*, by sacrifices, austerities and
> alms-giving, and goes to the Supreme Original State.

Commentary

The chapter concludes by presenting the two ways by which this world can be abandoned, the path of liberation obviously recommended.[11] The chapter ends with the word *ādi*, referring to the 'Supreme Original State', which suggests that perhaps the soul has arrived in this world after leaving that original, natural and supreme home.

---

[11] These two ways are also described in the *Bṛhad āraṇyaka Upaniṣad*, 6.2.1–16, and *Chāndogya Upaniṣad*, 5.3.1–5.10.8.

Chapter 9
The Vision of the Supreme – Part II

The Most Mysterious Knowledge

> 1 The blessed Lord said: I shall now reveal to you who are devoid of envy, the greatest mystery of all; knowledge and its realization; knowing this you will be freed from inauspiciousness. 2 This is a royal science, a royal mystery, the supreme purifier, experienced directly, it conforms to *dharma*, pleasant to act upon and eternal. 3 O Parantapa, those devoid of faith in this *dharma*, will not attain me but return to the path of repeated transmigration and death.

Commentary

Having descended to some extent during Chapter 8 the 'second tier' point of view, the discussion here returns to the 'third tier'. Kṛṣṇa opens by complimenting Arjuna for his lack of envy, the qualification based upon which he is able to acquire the knowledge about to be delivered; this is perceived or grasped directly, by means of *pratyakṣa* or direct perception. It may well be that this kind of *pratyakṣa* is a direct experience or vision of divinity, as may also be expressed by the term *darśana*. This knowledge conforms to *dharma* as it furthers the performance of duties in the context of the *Varṇāśrama* framework. However, *dharma* is also mentioned in a different context befitting the third tier, and as such it refers to the path of devotion or *bhakti*. There is a noteworthy resemblance between the structure of the present chapter and Chapter 7; both chapters begin with a short section glorifying the knowledge about to be delivered, and both second sections delineate the nature of divinity, its all-pervasiveness and its complex relation to the world of phenomena. Both third sections differentiate between the non-devotees and the devotees, and expand on the nature of the devoted, and both fourth sections emphasize Kṛṣṇa's equality to all. From the viewpoint of this tier there exist those who serve the Supreme Person without jealousy and are devoted to him, and on the other hand there are the faithless, sceptics and cynics, who are doomed to drown in the ocean of *saṁsāra*. Another notable feature of this tier is that one's identity is constructed by his or her relationships with the Supreme Person. This is different from the first tier, where identity is constructed and defined through adherence to *dharma*, or from the second one, where identity is constructed through self-restraint and detachment. As it is the personal relationships with the Supreme Person which enable one to get established in the 'third tier', he who is not jealous of the Supreme Person, who has faith in him and is devoted to him, comes closer to him, is freed from inauspiciousness and ultimately attains *mokṣa*. Naturally, the opposite is true as well.

The Supreme Person is Simultaneously Immanent in and Transcendent to the Material World

> 4 I pervade the entire world in my unmanifest form; all beings rest in me, but
> I do not rest in them. 5 And yet all beings do not rest in me; see my mystic
> splendour! I sustain beings but rely not on them; my very self is the cause of
> their being. 6 As the great wind that goes everywhere is eternally contained
> within space, know that similarly all beings are contained in me. 7 O Kaunteya,
> at the end of the vast cycle of time, all beings enter my material nature, and
> with the beginning of a new cycle, I create them again. 8 Resting on my own
> nature I create again and again this entire host of beings, who are involuntarily
> activated by that nature. 9 These actions do not bind me, O Dhanañjaya, as I am
> indifferent and unattached to all these activities. 10 Material nature creates all
> beings, moving and nonmoving alike, under my supervision. This, O Kaunteya,
> makes the world revolve.

Commentary

The Supreme Person is simultaneously immanent and transcendent; being immanent, the Supreme is very close; he is present everywhere in his invisible form and all living entities are not only supported by him, but are controlled by him through the agency of nature which he supervises. The entire world is contained within him just as the wind is contained within space, but at the same time, the various entities do not rest upon him directly but are helplessly controlled by nature. Nevertheless, he maintains a distinct and separate mode of existence; while resting on his nature alone, indifferent and unattached to worldly activities under the *guṇas*, he is unreachable and veiled from the world by his deluding power, consisting of the three *guṇas*. Viewed thus, the world is directly ruled by nature, and only indirectly governed by the supreme. These significant theological statements point to the rich and complex concept of divinity hereby presented. It seems that in this section Kṛṣṇa offers Arjuna a vision or *darśana* through a direct experience, having ceased to present rational arguments, and it appears that Chapters 7 and 9 play a crucial role in Arjuna's acceptance of Kṛṣṇa's message. Arjuna does not argue nor questions any longer, rather, it seems that he is fascinated by the might of the divine vision revealed to him, he listens carefully to Kṛṣṇa's words, and simply absorbs what he hears. His response to this revelatory experience will follow at the beginning of Chapter 10.

The Demons and the Great Souls

11 Fools deride me when I take on a human form, ignorant of my higher nature
as the great Lord of all beings. 12 Theirs are vain aspirations, vain actions, vain
knowledge and absence of mind. Thus their nature is demonic, immersed in evil
and illusion. 13 But those great souls whose nature is immersed in the divine,
worship me intently, O Pārtha, knowing me to be the imperishable source of
all beings. 14 Ever striving to glorify me with fortitude, bowing down to me
in devotion, they are ever absorbed in worshiping me. 15 Others, offering me
the sacrifice of knowledge, worship me as unity, as diversity, or as variously
manifested and facing all directions. 16 I am the ritual, I am the sacrifice, I am
the offering to the ancestors, I am the healing herb, I am the *mantra*, I am the
ghee,[1] I am the fire and I am the oblation. 17 The father of the whole world am I,
the mother, the supporter, the grandfather, the object of knowledge, the purifier,
the sacred syllable *Oṁ*, and the *Ṛg*, *Sāma*, and *Yajur Veda*. 18 I am the goal, the
sustainer, the master, the witness, the abode, the refuge, the well-wishing friend,
the origin, the dissolution, the foundation, the resting place and the eternal seed.
19 I radiate heat, I withhold and send forth the rain, I am immortality and death
too, and I am the existent and nonexistent, O Arjuna. 20 The knowers of the three
Vedas, who drink the *soma* juice become purified of their evils, and worship me
through sacrifices whose aim is to attain heaven.[2] Having reached the meritorious
world of Indra, the lord of the gods, they enjoy the celestial joys of the gods.
21 Having then enjoyed the vast world of heaven, their merit exhausted, they
reenter the world of the mortals. Thus, those following *Vedic dharma*, who yearn
to fulfil their desires, attain in this way only the temporary and impermanent. 22
But those whose consciousness is fixed on me alone, worshiping me, and ever
absorbed in me, to them I carry what they lack, and preserve what they already
possess. 23 Even those devoted to other gods, who worship these deities in good
faith, actually worship me alone, O Kaunteya, although they follow not the right
procedure. 24 For I alone am the master and enjoyer of all sacrifices; some fail
to recognize and truly know me as such, and hence they fall down. 25 Those
devoted to the gods go to the gods, those devoted to the ancestors go to the
ancestors, those devoted to ghosts and spirits go to the ghosts and spirits, and
those who are devoted to me will surely come to me.

1 Clarified butter.

2 It seems that the worship of Kṛṣṇa mentioned here is indirect; this also corresponds to the parallel section in Chapter 7, where those who worship the gods are said to reach them. See 7.23.

Commentary

Deep devotional sentiments are expressed here and these are representative of the third tier; accordingly, those who discard Kṛṣṇa's divinity possess a demonic nature, and as such their hope for redemption is lost. Conversely, there are those who are devoted to the Supreme Person, worship him in great devotion and view his immanence in various ways; moreover, they gain intimate relationships with him, so much so that he carries what they lack and preserves what they have. Apparently, they reach him after death and gain liberation in his proximity. Kṛṣṇa criticizes the *Vedic* sacrifices whose goal is the mere fulfillment of worldly desires and, as opposed to release from the cycle of birth and death, they result in merely transient fruits. As these yield but heavenly enjoyments, the performers of those sacrifices return to this world of mortals after the heavenly pleasures terminate. This section is of an apparent *Upaniṣadic* character in that it presents an abstraction of the sacrificial ingredients[3] and, moreover, in that it accentuates the sacrifice of knowledge. However, here the supreme in person is himself the ritual, the sacrifice, the offering, the *mantra*, the ghee, the fire and the oblation, as well as the three *Vedas* along with the sacred syllable *Oṁ*. Whoever attains this vision worships the supreme not only directly but also through the performance of *Vedic* sacrifices. Conversely, those who regard the *Vedic* sacrifices as mere means of satisfying their desires, serve the supreme indirectly and without complete and true understanding. Therefore they do not attain proximity to him, nor liberation, but merely the heavenly planets of the gods. Even the latter are attained for a limited time only, as at the exhaustion of the sacrificial results the performers fall back to earth. This section also presents a theistic version of the *Upaniṣadic* idea of the ancestors' path and the gods' path; accordingly, those who follow the *Vedic dharma* enjoy heaven, but then return to the human world of the mortals, whereas those who worship the Supreme Person come to him, never to return again. However, in the *Upaniṣadic* version, those who reach the ancestors return to rebirth, whereas those who reach the gods progress further on to reach *Brahman* and liberation.[4] The *Upaniṣadic* character of this section is also expressed in the criticism of the *Vedic* sacrifices, whose problematic nature is viewed here in a new light: the problem lies not with the attachment for the sacrificial fruits, rather with the underlying understanding; when one sacrifices with the right understanding, i.e. knowing the ritual to be identical with Kṛṣṇa himself, he attains devotion unto him. However, when one takes the *Vedic* sacrifice to be different from Kṛṣṇa, he attains merely temporary heavenly pleasures.

---

[3] An example of the abstraction of sacrificial ingredients may be found in *Bṛhadāraṇyaka Upaniṣad* 1.1.1 where the sacrificial horse is given a cosmogonic interpretation.

[4] E.g. *Bṛhadāraṇyaka Upaniṣad*, 6.2.15–16, *Chāndogya Upaṇiṣad*, 5.3.2.

Pure Devotion

> 26 When one offers me in devotion a leaf, a flower, a fruit or water, I accept that loving offering, as it is rendered out of a pure heart. 27 Whatever you do, whatever you eat, whatever you offer in sacrifice, whatever you give away and whatever austerity you may practice, O Kaunteya, do it as an offering unto me. 28 Thus you will be freed from the bondage of actions, along with its auspicious and inauspicious fruits. Wholly absorbed in *yoga* of renunciation, you shall become liberated and come to me. 29 I am equal to all beings, as I hate no one nor is anyone dear to me; however, those who worship me devoutly are in me, and I am in them too. 30 Even the habitual evil-doer, when fixed in devotion to me, is to be held a saint, for his conviction is right. 31 Quickly does he become established on the path of *dharma* and attains everlasting peace. O Kaunteya, know for certain that my devotee shall never be destroyed! 32 Those who take refuge in me, be they of lowly origin, women, merchants and even servants; even they may attain the highest destination. 33 And how much the more the saintly brahmins and the enlightened and devoted kings! Therefore, having reached this temporary and miserable world, devote yourself to me. 34 Always think of me and become my devotee, worship me and pay homage unto me; thus yoked to me and intent on me as your highest goal, you shall come to me.

Commentary

This section undoubtedly comprises one of the peaks of the entire *Bhagavad Gītā*, in that it presents the ideal of devotion or *bhakti* to the Supreme Person as open to all, and as the direct means of establishing personal relations with him. Here it is not knowledge or intellectual ability which is necessary, nor complex sacrificial performance, nor austere *yoga* practice, rather all that is required for achieving these personal relations with the Supreme Person is a pure heart. Kṛṣṇa commences by declaring that he accepts a sacrifice offered by a pure-hearted and devoted person, even though it may be as simple as a leaf, a flower, a fruit or water. He then requests Arjuna to perform all his worldly activities as a service unto himself, and promises a consequent release from all shackles of action, both good and bad. Kṛṣṇa then assures his being equal to all, but at the same time highlights his intimate relationships with those who are devoted and dedicated to him. The power of devotion is so strong that even the evil-doers are transformed into righteous people, and subsequently become established on the path of *dharma*. As opposed to the paths of *karma*[5] and *jñāna*, this path is open to all, including women, *vaiśyas* and *śūdras*; the path of *bhakti* may seem easier than the path of knowledge, which requires an intellectual capacity, easier than the path of *yoga* which requires austerity, and easier than the path of *karma* which necessitates ritualistic purity; as opposed to these three paths, *bhakti* seems to require no more

[5] In the *Vedic* ritualistic sense as opposed to *karma yoga*.

than a pure heart and sincere feelings towards the Supreme Person. However, the path of *bhakti* is in a sense more difficult since intellectual capacity as well as the capacity to perform austerities or sacrifices may cover or disguise various negative emotions directed towards the Supreme Person. Accordingly, jealousy, anger, religious utilitarianism and so forth, become sooner apparent than in the practice of the other paths and, as such, it may be difficult to progress on this path without giving these up, through undergoing a change of heart, a task which is not at all easy, and which requires a deep and real coping with the depths of one's mind and heart.

The question of evil,[6] which, despite various attempts, has not so far received a satisfactory solution, has by now received its final and fullest answer. Accordingly, devotion to the Supreme Person relieves one from the reactions to all one's deeds, both good and bad.[7] That is because the devotee carries out all his activities in the mood of service rendered unto the Supreme Person, who, in turn, becomes his devotee's patron and as such accepts responsibility for the deeds of his servant; naturally the latter is exempt from all responsibility or reactions to his deeds, be they good or bad. As such, the practice of *bhakti* includes relief from one's *karma*, which not only sanctifies the practitioner, but establishes him or her on the path of *dharma*. A question may be raised; isn't the Supreme Person affected by the *karma* he accepts from his devotee? The answer already given is that the supreme is not tainted nor bound by actions, and apparently is not affected by *karma*.[8] As for the nature of worship delineated here, it seems that this doesn't refer to liturgical temple worship, rather to a kind of 'practical worship' expressed through everything Arjuna does; accordingly fighting, too, may be considered a service rendered in devotion and dedication to the Supreme Person. It would appear that two levels of devotion could be articulated: the first level[9] refers to acting in accordance with one's own nature, and dedicating the fruits of actions to the supreme, whereas the second and higher level is that described in the chapter's concluding verse;[10] it depicts a state of complete immersion in the Supreme Person, spontaneous and independent of one's nature, and seems to represent one of the peaks of the entire *Bhagavad Gītā*. This is so significant that it will be quoted again almost verbatim at the end of the *Bhagavad Gītā*'s epilogue.[11] The articulation of *bhakti* as expressed in the present section, allowing one to offer Kṛṣṇa not only practical labour but one's entire life, provides concrete reasons for the *Bhagavad Gītā*'s popularity and wide circulation. Moreover, everyone is invited to practice *bhakti*, including those of low birth. Kṛṣṇa declares that his devotees will not be lost, and

6 *Pāpa*.

7 This idea is very significant and as such appears again in the epilogue; see *BG* 18.66.

8 *BG* 4.14.

9 *BG* 9.27.

10 *BG* 9.34.

11 *BG* 18.65.

that may hint that his devotee, Arjuna, who is devoted to him, will win the battle. Finally Kṛṣṇa pleads Arjuna to devote himself completely to him, and promises that subsequently he shall reach him.

Chapter 10
Arjuna's Change of Heart and the Divine Manifestations

Kṛṣṇa Reveals his Mystic Splendour

1–2 The Blessed Lord said: Again, O mighty-armed Arjuna, as you are dear to me,
please hear my supreme words spoken for your benefit; neither the hosts of gods
nor the great seers know my origin, for in every respect, I am the source of the
gods and of the sages. 3 He who knows me as the unborn, as the beginningless
and as the great ruler of the world, that undeluded among mortals is freed from all
sins. 4–5 Enlightenment, knowledge, freedom from delusion, forbearance, truth,
self-control, tranquillity, happiness, distress, becoming and unbecoming, fear
and fearlessness, nonviolence, equanimity, satisfaction, austerity, charity, fame
and infamy, this diversity of existential modes of being springs from me alone.
6 The seven great ancient seers, and the four Manus from whom the world's
population originates, have their origin in me, born of my mind. 7 He who knows
in truth my splendour and mystic power, is fixed in unwavering *yoga* and thus
yoked with me; of this there is no doubt. 8 I am the source of all that exists; from
me everything emanates; the enlightened who thus know me, worship me with
all their hearts. 9 Those whose consciousness is absorbed in me, for whom I am
everything, enlighten one another about me, constantly speaking of me; thus
absorbed, they are delighted and content. 10 Those thus constantly absorbed in
me, who worship me with love, I endow with the understanding by which they
can come to me. 11 Out of compassion alone I, dwelling in their hearts, destroy
the darkness of their ignorance with the shining torch of knowledge.

Commentary

The Supreme Person cannot be empirically known since he is the source of everything; therefore one must rely on the supreme himself in order to know him. Kṛṣṇa explains to Arjuna how he can be known; as such he describes various states of existence, as well as the ancient sages and the Manus of whom the population of the universe was generated, all of them originating from him. Acceptance of the Supreme Person as the source of everything represents a state of enlightenment, and those who are thus enlightened are wholeheartedly devoted to him. It seems that this state of perception is not the result of a detached logical or scholarly enquiry, rather a type of knowledge resulting from dependence upon and dedication to the Supreme Person. Kṛṣṇa observes how much his devotees are happy in their devotion to him and adds that he himself, seeing their attempts to approach him, takes the initiative and destroys their ignorance by bestowing enlightenment upon them. Apparently, the Supreme Person does not bestow knowledge of himself freely upon all, rather it is a benediction bestowed upon those who are devoted to him. Moreover, bestowing this knowledge is a means for destroying the ignorance covering the devoted, a benediction which apparently is not bestowed upon the non-devoted. It seems that this close relation between devotion and knowledge is one of the *Bhagavad Gītā*'s central epistemological themes. It is quite possible that Kṛṣṇa's words about the removal of ignorance were directed at the last doubts which Arjuna may still have entertained. As such, this discussion is not merely theoretical, but may have well brought Arjuna to the point of waiving all further question or argument; it may well be that the time for his change of heart has arrived.

Arjuna's Change of Heart

> 12 Arjuna said: Your Honour is the Supreme *Brahman*, the Supreme Abode, the Supreme Purifier, the Eternal Divine Person, the Primal God, Unborn and All Pervading. 13 Thus have all the seers declared; the divine seer Nārada, Asita, Devala and Vyāsa, and indeed, now You Yourself declare it unto me. 14 O Keśava, I believe all that you are telling me is true. O Lord, neither the gods nor the demons know your appearance. 15 O Supreme Person, maintainer of all, Lord of all beings, God among gods, Master of the world, You Yourself know yourself through Yourself.

Commentary

Arjuna undergoes a conversion or a change of heart; as such he proclaims that he accepts as truth and without reservation all that Kṛṣṇa has said, and subsequently fully accepts his divinity. As part of his declaration, Arjuna says that not only did Kṛṣṇa delineate his divinity in this fashion, but that it was also declared by authorities such as Nārada, Asita, Devala and Vyāsa, and, as such, carries additional weight. This appears to be the core of the conversion which Arjuna is undergoing: the numerous arguments which were gradually raised led to the manifestation of Kṛṣṇa's divinity. Once Arjuna has attained that stage, with his consciousness fixed in the third tier, he absorbed this manifestation, accepted it as true, and at this point finally gave up all his arguments. From a wider perspective, it seems that Arjuna had, prior to this point, maintained numerous objections to Kṛṣṇa's ideas and doctrine, and as such could not have accepted his divinity. Gradually, however, through ascending step by step the internal ladder, Arjuna has accepted Kṛṣṇa's divinity, while gradually relinquishing familiarity in favour of devotion; it seems that the friend has turned into a disciple, and that the disciple has turned into a dedicated devotee. It appears that the experience of devotion and the ensuing acceptance of Kṛṣṇa's divinity is of an uncritical character, as Arjuna has given up his argumentative approach in favour of a state of satisfaction and immersion in a divine vision. Kṛṣṇa, on his part, while conferring mystical revelations on Arjuna, has not changed his basic position in regards to the war; he still requests Arjuna to fight, and it appears now that Arjuna accepts this and will do whatever he is asked to do.

The Divine Manifestations in the World

> 16 I beg you; describe fully your divine self-manifestations, in which you
> abide in the worlds and pervade them. 17 O *Yogī*, how may I always meditate
> upon you and know you? O Lord, in what different states of being can you be
> contemplated? 18 O Janārdana, please describe to me further and in its details
> your own supernal power, for I shall never be sated with hearing the nectar
> of your words. 19 The Blessed Lord said: So be it; I shall describe to you my
> main divine self-manifestations, as my plentitude is infinite. 20 I am the self, O
> Guḍākeśa, abiding in the heart of every being; I am the beginning, the middle,
> and the end of all beings. 21 Among the *Ādityas* I am Viṣṇu, of lights the radiant
> sun, of *Maruts*, Marīci am I and among stars, I am the moon. 22 Of the *Vedas* I
> am the *Sāma Veda*, of gods, I am Indra, among the senses I am the mind, and
> of beings I am consciousness. 23 Of the *Rudras* I am Śiva, of the *Yakṣasas* and
> *Rakṣasas* I am Kuvera, Of the *Vasus* I am fire, and among mountains, *Meru* I
> am. 24 O Pārtha, of priests know me to be the chief, Bṛhaspati. Of generals I am
> Skanda, and among bodies of water, I am the ocean. 25 Of the great seers I am
> Bhṛgu, of utterances I am the syllable *Oṁ*, of sacrifices I am the *Japa*–sacrifice,
> and among immovable beings the *Himālayas*. 26 Of all trees I am the *Aśvattha*,
> of the divine seers I am Nārada, of the *Gandharvas* I am Citraratha, and among
> perfected beings the sage Kapila. 27 Of horses know me to be Uccaiḥśravas, who
> sprung from nectar churned of the ocean, of princely elephants I am Airāvata,
> and the king among men. 28 Of weapons I am the thunderbolt, of cows I am the
> wish-fulfilling cow, in procreation Kandarpa, the god of love I am, and among
> serpents I am Vāsuki. 29 Of the *Nāgas* I am Ananta, of aquatics I am Varuṇa, of
> departed ancestors I am Aryamā and among those who tame I am Yama. 30 Of
> *Daityas* I am Prahlāda, of things countable I am time, of beasts I am the lion, and
> among birds Garuḍa I am. 31 Of purifiers I am the wind, of warriors I am Rāma,
> of sea monsters I am the *Makara*, and among rivers I am the Ganges, known as
> Jāhnavī. 32 Of creations I am the beginning, end and middle as well, O Arjuna. Of
> all types of knowledge, I am the knowledge of the self and among theoreticians I
> am logic. 33 Of letters I am the letter A, and of compounds the compound called
> *dvandva*; I alone am eternal time, and I am the creator, facing all directions. 34
> I am death, who snatches away everything, and the origin of things yet to be;
> among women I am fame, fortune, eloquence, memory, wisdom, steadfastness
> and patience. 35 Of *Vedic* chants I am the *Bṛhatsāma*, of meters the *Gāyatrī* I am,

of months I am *Mārgaśīrṣa*,[1] and among seasons, the flower-bearing spring. 36
Of means of cheating I am gambling, and I am the splendour of the splendid; I
am victory, I am the spirit of adventure, and I am the courage of the courageous.
37 Of the *Vṛṣṇis* I am Vāsudeva, of Pāṇḍu's sons I am Dhanañjaya; moreover, of
contemplative hermits I am Vyāsa, and of sages I am the sage Uśanā. 38 Of rulers
I am the rod of punishment, of those desiring victory I am the statesmanship;
of secret things I am silence, and I am the knowledge of the wise. 39 O Arjuna,
the seed of all beings is also me; indeed, nothing moving or unmoving exists
without me. 40 O Parantapa, there is no end to my divine manifestations; the
extent of my plenitude have I described through examples only. 41 Whatever
creation manifests supernal splendour you should understand it to originate from
my splendour. 42 But what is the point for you of this extensive description? I
support this entire world with a mere single fraction of mine!

Commentary

Kṛṣṇa describes his various manifestations in this world, in response to Arjuna's request. This is an additional revelation offered in the *Bhagavad Gītā*, a revelation of immanent divinity as representative of the essence and the peak of all phenomena. Ultimately, Kṛṣṇa asserts, these details are minor, as he maintains the whole universe with but a fraction of his power.

[1] November–December.

Chapter 11
The Cosmic Revelation

Arjuna's Request

1 Arjuna said: You have revealed to me for my benefit that supreme secret,
the nature of the self; hearing your words, my illusion has been dispelled. 2 O
Lotus petal-eyed Kṛṣṇa, I have heard from you in detail of the becoming and
dissolving of all creatures, and of your own eternal greatness. 3 I now desire to
see your supernal form, just as you have described yourself, O Supreme Lord,
O Supreme Person. 4 O Lord, if you think that I can bear this sight, please reveal
your imperishable self to me, O Master of Mystic Power. 5 The Blessed Lord
said: O Pārtha, behold my forms, by hundreds and thousands, infinite variety,
divine, and replete with colours and shapes. 6 O Bhārata, behold the Ādityas,
Vasus, Rudras, the two Aśvins, the Maruts, and behold many wonderful forms
never seen before! 7 O Guḍākeśa, behold now in my body the entire universe,
along with its moving and unmoving beings, all in one place, and whatever else
you wish to see. 8 But you cannot see me with your own eyes; I therefore grant
you a divine vision. Behold my Majestic Splendour!

Commentary

Arjuna has by now accepted Kṛṣṇa's divinity and has clearly declared that;[1] following this he heard about Kṛṣṇa's various manifestations in the world. Arjuna is naturally curious to experience a more tangible demonstration of Kṛṣṇa's divinity, a more direct revelation or what may be considered 'a classical theophany'. However, he justly expresses a concern, and inquires whether he will be capable of bearing such a display without losing his mental balance. Arjuna's somewhat official addressing of Kṛṣṇa as 'Lord' also forewarns of the coming events, since in the face of the spectacle of Kṛṣṇa's divinity, Arjuna will not be able to maintain the friendly relationships held up until now, nor even the teacher–disciple relationship. Kṛṣṇa is about to satisfy Arjuna's request, and to that end he provides him with a special sense of sight, which will enable him to see the entire universe as well as various divine manifestations all in his own body, while standing in Arjuna's proximity.

---

[1] 10.12–15.

The Revelation

9 Sañjaya said: O king,[2] having thus spoken, the great master of mystics Hari revealed to Pārtha his supernal majestic form. 10 Of countless mouths and eyes, of countless wonderful revelations, of countless divine ornaments, of countless divine weapons ready for battle. 11 Clad in celestial garlands and garments, anointed with divine perfumes, God whose whole being is wonderful, infinite and turned towards all directions. 12 If a thousand suns were to rise at once in the sky, their splendour would have resembled the brilliance of that great form. 13 At that time the son of Pāṇḍu saw the entire universe with its diversity and variety united in the body of the God of gods. 14 Then, overwhelmed with astonishment and his hair standing on end, Dhanañjaya bowed his head over folded hands to the Supreme Person and spoke: 15 Arjuna said: O Lord, I see all the gods in your body, and a variety of creatures assembled, the sovereign god Brahmā seated on his lotus seat, all the seers as well as the divine serpents. 16 I see you everywhere in an infinite form, having unlimited arms, bellies, mouths and eyes; I behold in you no end, no middle and no beginning, O Lord of all, whose form is the entire world. 17 Difficult as it is to behold you, I see you clearly adorned with a diadem, armed with a club and a disc, and spreading clouds of splendour on all sides; your blazing sun like fiery radiance is immeasurable! 18 You are the Imperishable and the Supreme Object of Knowledge; you are the Ultimate Foundation of all, and you are the Eternal Protector of the Eternal *Dharma*. Indeed, I deem you to be the Everlasting Person. 19 Without beginning, middle or end, of infinite power, of unlimited arms, the sun and the moon your eyes, I thus behold you, whose mouth blazes like the sacrificial fire; with your radiance, you burn this entire world. 20 You alone fill the space between heaven and earth, and pervade all directions; O great one, the three worlds tremble at seeing this terrible and wonderful form of yours. 21 The hosts of gods enter into you, some terrified, praising you with folded hands; the throngs of great seers and the perfected beings glorify you with *Vedic* chants, crying hail! 22 The Rudras, Ādityas, Vasus and the Sādhyas, the Viśva devas, the two Aśvins, the Maruts and the ancestors, the throngs of Gandharvas, Yakṣas, Asuras, and perfected ones, all behold you in astonishment. 23 O Mighty Armed one, at the sight of your great form, of many mouths and eyes, of many arms, thighs and feet, of many bellies and of many terrible tusks, the worlds tremble, and so do I. 24 O Viṣṇu, beholding you touch the sky, flaming in many colours, your great mouth gaping and your enormous eyes blazing, my whole being trembles; neither firmness nor peace of mind can I find. 25 Watching your mouths of many terrible teeth like unto the fire of destruction that brings about the world's end, I lose direction and find no refuge. O Lord of gods! O refuge of the worlds, have mercy! 26–27 All Dhṛtarāṣṭra's sons accompanied by hosts of kings, sovereigns of the earth, and Bhīṣma, Droṇa, Karṇa with our chief warriors, rush into your mouths full of

2 Addressing Dhṛtarāṣṭra.

dreadful teeth. Some are seen between your teeth, their heads crushed. 28 As the many furious rivers flow towards the ocean, so do the world's heroes enter your blazing mouths. 29 As moths rush into burning fire for their destruction, similarly these people hasten into your mouths for their ruination. 30 O Viṣṇu! You fiercely lick your lips on all sides, swallowing all the worlds in your flaming mouths! Your blazing radiance burns the whole world filled with your glory! 31 Who are you of terrible form? Reveal it to me, I beseech! I fall at your feet and beg for your mercy, O best of gods. O Primeval One, I desire to understand Your Honor, as your purpose is not clear to me. 32 The Blessed Lord said: Time I am, the great destroyer of the worlds, and I have come to annihilate all assembled here; even without you, these warriors arrayed in opposing ranks shall not survive. 33 Therefore arise and reap glory! Your enemies conquered, you shall enjoy the flourishing kingdom. By me alone are they already slain; therefore be but an instrument in my hands, O Savyasācin. 34 Droṇa, Bhīṣma, Jayadratha, Karṇa, and other heroes have I already destroyed. Fight! Destroy them without hesitating! You will conquer your enemies in this battle.

Commentary

A theophany at its best is herein presented; it is no doubt one of the *Bhagavad Gītā*'s peaks, and an important revelation in terms of world religions. Kṛṣṇa, Arjuna's close friend who has become his *guru*, turns now into the mighty universal god Viṣṇu; as such, the friendly and relaxed discourse between the two changes into excited exclamations and declarations by Arjuna. Beholding the awesome, enormous and terrifying exhibition of divine power, Arjuna finds it hard to retain his composure and resolve. In the course of this demonstration Arjuna sees how most warriors present are to be killed by this universal figure. Viṣṇu declares that he is time, and as such came to annihilate everything; since his prediction and plan is that most warriors be killed, Arjuna is commanded to play the role of a mere instrument in his hands, fight and attain victory.

Arjuna's Speech

35 Sañjaya said: having heard Keśava's words, frightened and trembling, offering obeisances to Kṛṣṇa again and again with folded hands, Arjuna spoke in his great turmoil. 36 Arjuna said: It is only proper, O Hṛṣīkeśa, that the world rejoices and delights in your praise, that the demons flee in all directions, and that all the throngs of perfected ones bow to you. 37 O Great Soul, why should they not bow down before you? You are the primeval creator, greater even than Brahmā! Infinite you are! Lord of the gods, refuge of the universe! You are eternal, that which exists, that which exists not, and that which is beyond both! 38 You are the Original God, the Primal Person; for the whole world you are the Supreme Resting-Place. You are the Knower, the Known, and the Supreme Abode. You

whose form knows no limits, pervade the whole world. 39 You are Vāyu the wind
god, Yama the god of death, Agni the god of fire, Varuṇa the god of the oceans,
the Moon god, Brahmā lord of creatures, and the Primal grandfather. I fall at your
feet again and again, a thousand times and yet again! 40 My homage from the
front! My homage from behind! I offer my homage to you from all directions!
Of unlimited vigour and infinite might you are! You pervade everything and thus
you are everything! 41 Rashly thinking you to be my comrade, I have addressed
you 'O Kṛṣṇa, O Yādava, O my Friend' without knowing this greatness of yours.
I have done so in absence of mind, or perhaps out of sheer affection. 42 At times
I have jested, at times I have treated you disrespectfully, sometimes we enjoyed
ourselves together, lay on the same bed, sat together or dined together; and
not only privately, O Kṛṣṇa, but with others as well. O Immeasurable One, I
beg Your forgiveness! 43 You are the Universal Father of the moving and the
unmoving alike; a most venerable *guru* are you, unequalled and to be worshiped
by all. How could anyone surpass you, O Lord of Immeasurable Power! 44
Therefore, prostrating myself at your feet, I pay obeisance and beg your mercy.
O Worshipful Lord, forgive me as a father his son, as a friend excuses his friend,
or as a lover absolves his beloved. O God, bear with me! 45 Having seen that
which has never before been seen I am thrilled, but my heart trembles in fear;
please reveal to me again the form I have known, O Lord of gods, repose of the
world. 46 I beg to see you again just as before, crowned with a diadem, armed
with the club, discus in hand; I entreat you to assume once again your four
handed-form, O Thousand Armed One, O embodiment of all.

Commentary

Arjuna has by now not only satisfied his curiosity as to Kṛṣṇa's divinity, but he feels elated at the sight of that marvellous manifestation of supernal power. At the same time he is in a perturbed emotional state and asks to see Kṛṣṇa as he had known him prior to the revelation – as a friend in a human form. Apparently, the revelation caused a transition from a friendly relationship to one of respect and dread towards Kṛṣṇa in his supernal form. In the friendly setting Arjuna and Kṛṣṇa had expressed their mutual friendship informally, whereas following the revelation, the state of friendship was replaced, on Arjuna's part, by astonishment, wonder, fear, reverence, submission, a loss of identity, confusion and a barely controllable mental turmoil. Arjuna wishes to bow to the Supreme Person again and again, and to praise his greatness and power; moreover, he regrets his previous familiar and informal behaviour towards Kṛṣṇa, not realizing who he truly was, and begs his forgiveness. Apparently, both Arjuna and Kṛṣṇa prefer the informal friendly exchange to the formal reverential mood, and moreover, the latter is somewhat alien to the prevailing mood of the *Bhagavad Gītā*, which is relatively peaceful and discursive. Notably, the emotions aroused in Arjuna in face of the divine revelation were not of affection, love or devotion but of distant awe and respect. In this emotional state, Arjuna regrets and apologizes for his previous informal dealings with Kṛṣṇa, which were an expression of fraternity and comradeship. Arjuna had his wish fulfilled, but it is doubtful whether he would have asked for that experience repeated.

Conclusion: Only by Devotion can the Supreme Person be Seen as He is and be Reached

> 47 The Blessed Lord said: out of my mercy towards you, Arjuna, and by my own mysterious potency, this supreme form has been manifested. This universal form of mine, of splendour, unlimited and primeval, was never before revealed to another but yourself. 48 Not by performing *Vedic* sacrifices or chanting hymns, not by acts of charity, by ceremonial rituals or awesome austerities, can anyone other than you among humans see me in such a form, O Kuru hero. 49 Be not perturbed or confused, on seeing this dreadful form of mine. Be of good cheer again, worry not and behold again the form of mine that you have known. 50
> Sañjaya said: having thus spoken to Arjuna, Vāsudeva revealed again his own familiar form; assuming again his gentle appearance, that great soul calmed the frightened Arjuna. 51 Arjuna said: beholding your beautiful and benevolent human form, O Janārdana, I am now composed, and my mind restored. 52 The Blessed Lord said: difficult is it indeed to behold the form that you have seen; in fact, even the gods are ever anxious to gain a vision of it. 53 Not by studying the *Vedas*, not by austerity, not by charity nor by sacrifice can I be seen in the manner you have seen me. 54 Only by undivided devotion, O Arjuna, can I be known and seen as I am in truth, and thus be attained. 55 He who acts for my sake, who accepts me as the Supreme, who is devoted to me, having abandoned both attachment and enmity towards all creatures, he will come to me, O Pāṇḍava.

Commentary

The chapter ends by reinforcing the *Bhagavad Gītā*'s central theme of *bhakti* or devotion. Kṛṣṇa says that the customary ritualistic and ascetic activities are insufficient for knowing and reaching him, and apparently, experiencing a revelation such as the one Arjuna has just experienced is not a recommended method either. The conclusion is that personal devotion is the best way to know Kṛṣṇa, to see him and to reach him. As such, the proceeding chapter turns to the topic of devotion.

Chapter 12
Stages of Devotion

Which is Better: the Worship of the Supreme Person or the Worship of *Brahman*?

1 Arjuna said: There are those who worship you, devoted to you and constantly absorbed in you, while there are others who worship the imperishable and unmanifest *Brahman*; who among them, is the most advanced in *yoga*? 2 The Blessed Lord said: Those whose minds are fixed on me, who are constantly absorbed in me, and worship me with deep faith, I consider them the most advanced in *yoga*. 3–4 But those who worship the imperishable, the inexplicable, the unmanifest, the all-pervading and inconceivable, the steady, fixed and firm – who, by subduing the various senses have attained complete equanimity and are concerned with the welfare of all – they indeed attain me. 5 The pains taken by those whose minds are absorbed in the unmanifest are greater, for the unmanifest goal is difficult indeed to attain for those who dwell in a body. 6–7 Conversely, those who regard me as the supreme and offer all their activities unto me, who meditate on me and worship me through undistracted *yoga*, for them I am the saviour from the ocean of *saṁsāra* and death. O Pārtha, I appear for them without delay as they have given me their heart.

Commentary

Arjuna explicitly requests a comparison between the path of devotion and the path of realizing impersonal *Brahman*, and asks which of the two is better. The tension between the two paths of spiritual realization is a basic theme in *Vedāntin* thought, and finds its expression, inter alia, in the medieval dispute between Śaṅkara and Rāmānuja, or between the *Advaita* and the *Vaiṣṇava* traditions. Those who accept the personal conception of divinity as supreme, consider *Brahman* realization to be a valid spiritual attainment leading to liberation, but still inferior to the complete realization of the Supreme Person through devotion. On the other hand, those who accept the impersonal concept of divinity as supreme, regard devotion to the Supreme Person as a preliminary spiritual stage intended to enable those who are still in need of concrete objects of worship, to gradually reach the unmanifest, subtle, ubiquitous and Impersonal *Brahman*. Since the *Bhagavad Gītā* simultaneously furthers both paths, and since the last chapters have focused on personal divinity and devotion, a comparison of the two paths is warranted. The question is clear, and so is the answer given; Kṛṣṇa begins by saying that those devoted to him as the Supreme Person are more advanced than those adhering to the knowledge of Impersonal *Brahman*. Those aiming at spiritual perfection through knowledge of *Brahman* will be successful too, but their way is more arduous since their goal is elusive, and since Impersonal *Brahman* is difficult to conceptualize by those conditioned by the physical. Kṛṣṇa emphasizes that for his devotees he is the saviour from *saṁsāra*, and proceeds to deepen the discussion of personal devotion through presenting the 'ladder of devotion'.

The Ethical Ladder of Devotion

> 8 Fix your mind on me alone, and absorb your consciousness in me; thus you shall surely abide in me. 9 If you cannot fix your consciousness steadily upon me, then aspire to reach me through repeated *yoga* practice, O Dhanañjaya. 10 If you are incapable even of that, embrace the path of action, for which I am the highest goal, since by acting for me you shall attain perfection. 11 But if you are even unable to follow this path of refuge in me through acts devoted to me, then give up the fruits of all your actions, thus restraining yourself. 12 Knowledge is superior to practice, meditation is superior to knowledge, and relinquishing the fruits of actions is higher than meditation, as tranquility soon follows such relinquishment.

Commentary

This section articulates the ladder principle underlying the entire *Bhagavad Gītā*, composing its structure along with the three levels of reality. The description descends from the top downwards, as opposed to the ladder presented from Chapter 2 onwards, depicting the ladder stages from bottom upwards. In terms of the three levels or tiers, the present discussion starts at the third tier representing immersion in the experience of divinity, down to the second tier depicting the endeavour made by those still bound by matter in their striving for liberation, and thence further down to the first tier. The highest state[1] is that of immersion in the Supreme Person, and as it is spontaneous, it does not require any external restraints; as such it may be called the stage of spontaneous devotion. The lower state[2] is that of *abhyāsa* or ongoing practice, and as opposed to the highest state, it is characterized by various *yogic* principles, rules and restraints. As *bhakti* here takes the form of a *yoga* practice, it may be considered the stage of *bhakti yoga*. The next stage[3] is activity dedicated to Kṛṣṇa; this activity seems to be activity according to *dharma*; as such, it is performed according to the nature of the performer, and its fruits are offered to the supreme. It may be considered *karma yoga*, and Chapters 3 and 5 deal with the subject at length. The following and

1 12.8.
2 12.9.
3 12.10.

lower stage[4] furthers the relinquishment of the fruits of action; this is a type of self-restraint and it naturally brings tranquillity. As opposed to the higher stage, which furthers the offering of action's fruits to the supreme, this stage furthers a general relinquishment and as such is considered lower. A lower stage still is meditation, knowledge is the next, and eventually there is practice. It does not appear to be the *yoga* practice mentioned at the second step of the ladder, and it may well be the practice of the *Veda*.[5] We may have here an unequivocal statement in regards to the supremacy of *karma yoga* over *jñāna yoga*;[6] this is consistent not only with the general mood of the *Bhagavad Gītā*, but with the present chapter as well, according to which the path of active work or service is recommended over the path of abstract contemplation.

The Devotee who is Dear to the Supreme Person

> 13–14 He who hates no living being, is friendly and compassionate, is devoid of possessiveness and egoism, equal in distress and happiness, forbearing towards others, a *yogī* who is always contented, self-controlled and of firm resolution, whose mind and consciousness are absorbed in me and is a devotee of mine, he is dear to me. 15 He by whom no one is agitated nor is he agitated by anyone, who is free from joy, impatience, fear and distress, he is dear to me. 16 He who dependent on nothing, is pure, adept, uninvolved, free from misery and anxiety, who has abandoned personal ambition and is a devotee of mine, is dear to me. 17 He who neither rejoices nor is disgusted, neither laments nor yearns, renouncing the auspicious and inauspicious alike, and is filled with devotion, is dear to me. 18–19 He who is alike towards friend and foe, and faces in like manner honour and dishonour, cold and heat, happiness and distress, free from attachment, to whom blame and praise are the one, satisfied under any circumstance, homeless, of a steady mind and full of devotion, such a person is dear to me. 20 Those devoted to me, who worship this eternal path of *dharma* thus described, faithful and accepting me as the Supreme, are very, very dear to me.

Commentary

Kṛṣṇa describes those devoted to him in great detail, praises their qualities and stresses how dear they are to him. On the one hand the devotees renounce the world at least internally, and develop indifference and equanimity towards it, while on the other they gain personal relationships with the Supreme Person, and become very dear to him. This section summarizes the second and middle section of the

---

4 12.11.

5 See Johannes Van Buitenen, *The Bhagavadgītā in the Mahābhārata* (Chicago and London, 1981), note 4 to Chapter 12, p. 168.

6 Loc. cit.

Bhagavad Gītā which is comprised of Chapters 7–12, and which deals extensively with divinity and the ideal of devotion. The following chapters support the idea of devotion through propounding knowledge in terms of the *Sāṅkhya* and *Vedānta* traditions.

Chapter 13
The Vision of the Supreme in the Heart

The Six Questions, the Field and the Knower of the Field

> 0 Arjuna said: O Keśava, I wish to know about material nature,[1] the conscious
> entity,[2] the field and the knower of the field, knowledge and the object
> of knowledge.[3] 1 The blessed Lord said: This body is known as the field, O
> Kaunteya, and one who knows it, is declared by the wise to be the knower of
> the field. 2 You should know me as the knower of the field as well, situated
> in all fields, O Bhārata. I deem knowledge of the field and of the knower of
> the field to be knowledge indeed. 3 Hear from me in summary what this field
> and its nature is, how it transforms and comes into being, who the knower of
> the field is, and what his powers are. 4 Seers have chanted this in many *Vedic*
> hymns in varied ways, as well as in the *Brahmasūtra* aphorisms, all of them
> authoritative and well-substantiated. 5–6 The great elements, the concept of ego,
> the intelligence and the unmanifest, the ten senses and the additional sense, the
> five sense objects, attraction and repulsion, happiness and distress, the aggregate,
> consciousness and inner conviction – all serve to sum up the nature of the field
> and its transformations.

Commentary

Having dealt extensively with the subject of devotion in the previous six chapters, the discussion assumes now a different character; it becomes more theoretical and closer to the *Vedānta* and *Sāṅkhya* mode of discourse. In a sense, the text now descends from the third tier which has occupied the previous chapters into the second tier; as such, the present discussion is more concerned with the living entity's entanglement in *saṁsāra* and the means of its release. Having examined reality in the previous chapters from the third tier's higher perspective, the text has been now enriched with a higher point of view; as such, it has attained a state of maturity which was absent from the first six chapters.

The chapter opens with Arjuna's six questions,[4] and in the present section the third and forth questions are addressed; these two questions are concerned with the

---

[1] *Prakṛti*.

[2] *Puruṣa*.

[3] The first verse is absent from some *BG* editions and was, therefore, following Zaehner, labeled no. 0.

[4] 13.0.

field and the knower of the field. Accordingly the soul requires a field of activity by which it can express itself in worldly life, and this field is the body which dictates a particular type of involvement in the world. Normally, seeds are sown in the field and later produce fruits; similarly the performance of a human action resembles the planting of a seed, in that it produces *karmic* fruits in the form of future reactions. The term field refers not only to the gross body, rather to its subtle or psychological aspects as well, and verses 5–6 list the various components comprising the field. The direct answer to the question of the knower of the field's identity is relatively simple; it is the self, i.e. the *ātman*. But Kṛṣṇa adds an interesting remark, and says that he, too, is the knower of the field, and moreover, that he is situated in all fields.[5] It seems that he is referring to the *paramātman*, also known as *antaryāmin*, who is the Supreme Person abiding along with each soul in every body, and accompanying it through its journey through *saṁsāra*. This form of divinity represents a midway position between the fully personal Supreme Person distinguished by unique qualities, and the impersonal divinity or *Brahman* who is undifferentiated and ubiquitous.

Knowledge

> 7 Absence of pride and arrogance, nonviolence, forbearance, honesty, attendance upon the *guru*, purity, firmness, self control, 8 lack of attraction to sense objects, absence of ego-notion, visioning the distress and evil of birth, death, old age and disease, 9 detachment, aloofness from sons, wife, home and the like, constant equanimity toward desired and undesired events, 10 single-minded devotion to me supported by *yoga*, preferring of solitary places and avoiding the crowds, 11 constantly contemplating knowledge of the self, envisioning the purpose of knowledge concerned with the truth – all these are declared knowledge, whereas all else is ignorance.

Commentary

In reply to Arjuna's request to know about knowledge,[6] Kṛṣṇa presents a list of inner qualities; these represent knowledge and their absence signifies the absence of knowledge or ignorance. The type of knowledge under discussion is not quantitative, intellectual or encyclopedic knowledge, rather it is knowledge of a different sort, acquired through inner transformation, and gained through an ethical training and character building. According to our model, it may be considered knowledge of the second tier or level, as it supports detachment and the development of a *yogic* vision. The emerging picture of the knowledgeable person is of a solitary ascetic, engaged in meditation while devoted to the Supreme Person. This raises a question:

---

[5] 13.2.

[6] *BG* 13.0; the 5th question.

how can Kṛṣṇa link this ideal of a solitary ascetic to the ideal of the vigorous and violent warrior which he expects Arjuna to be? The answer is to be found in the *yogic* concept mentioned in verse 10; accordingly, fulfilling one's duty as a way of actively serving the Supreme Person through fighting, comprises a form of *yoga*. This devotional *yoga* or *bhakti-yoga* involves the classical *yoga* components, but these are practiced not through solitary *yogic* postures and the like, rather through adherence to duty in the mood of service and devotion to the supreme. As such, forbearance will be manifested by Arjuna's restraining his own desires in favour of carrying out Kṛṣṇa's desires. The lack of ego will be expressed by his accepting the role of Kṛṣṇa's servant, and accepting the fighting of the war as his service. Similarly, endeavouring to be delivered from *saṁsāra* will be practiced by the relinquishment of attachment to sense objects in favour of offering the fruits of fighting to the supreme. Still, how can Arjuna practice nonviolence? The solution appears to be found in the instrumentality underlying the concept of devotion: in a sense, the Supreme Person is the one who really acts, whereas Arjuna is but an instrument in his hands; thus, the responsibility rests entirely with the supreme, who assumes responsibility for his servant's deeds carried under his instructions. This idea appears in Chapter 11 where Arjuna was asked to be but an instrument in the hands of the supreme,[7] and is further discussed in Chapter 18, which states that one who kills without maintaining a false conception of the self as the doer, does not in fact kill.[8] It is to be noted that while in general the traditional method requires the student to undergo a process of training and character building, a different course of events wherein knowledge precedes self-correction is possible under exceptional circumstances, such as sudden enlightenment or a divine revelation. An example for the latter is the revelation observed by Arjuna and described in the Chapter 11, resulting in his becoming humble, devoid of ego-notion and so forth.

The Object of Knowledge

> 12 I shall speak now about the object of knowledge, knowing which you shall attain the eternal. This is the beginningless *Brahman* and is subordinate to me;[9] it is said to have neither existence nor nonexistence. 13 Everywhere are its hands and legs, its eyes, heads and faces, and similarly, its ears which exist everywhere

---

7 *BG* 11.33.

8 *BG* 18.17.

9 Śaṅkara divides *anādimat paraṁ* translated as 'beginningless *Brahman*', whereas Rāmānuja divides *anādi matparaṁ* translated as 'beginningless and having me as the highest'. I follow the latter. See: *The Bhagavad Gītā With The Commentary of Ādi Śrī Śaṅkarācārya*, translated by A.M. Śāstri, 1897 (Chennai, 1995), p. 344, and *Śrī Rāmānuja Gītā Bhāṣya*, translated by Ādidevānanda Svāmī (Madras, 1991), pp. 437–439.

in the world; as such he is all-encompassing and aware of everything.[10] 14 Although devoid of perceptible qualities, he appears to possess them. Although he maintains everything, he is unattached to anything; he is freed from the *guṇas*, but nevertheless experiences the *guṇas*. 15 He exists inside and outside of all creatures, he is unmoving and moving, his subtlety makes him difficult to comprehend; he is at once remote and nearby. 16 Although he seems to be divided among all beings, he is actually undivided; he is to be known as the maintainer, devourer and creator of all creatures. 17 It is said that he is the light of lights situated beyond darkness, he is knowledge, the object of knowledge and the goal of knowledge; he abides in everyone's heart. 18 Thus have the field, knowledge and the object of knowledge been described briefly; knowing this, my devotee attains my nature.

Commentary

Regarding the question 'what is the object of knowledge',[11] Kṛṣṇa states that it is divinity. The answer opens by pointing directly at *Brahman*, but soon shifts to a description of the *Paramātman*, which is a personal form of divinity residing within the heart,[12] known also as *Antaryāmin*, and accompanying the embodied soul in its voyage through the world of *saṁsāra*.[13] This interesting idea is also encountered in the *Upaniṣads*, and it makes an important contribution to the diverse concepts of divinity found in the *Bhagavad Gītā*. This form is usually associated with *yogic* or mystic contemplation, and naturally evokes serene and peaceful moods, which are representative of quietist and mystic states of mind. According to *Vaiṣṇava* theology, the *Antaryāmin* or 'inner ruler' is a form of the deity that dwells in the human heart, guides it and accompanies it through the experiences of heaven and hell.[14] The *Kaṭha Upaniṣad*, Chapter 4, describes the personalized divinity quite explicitly:

4.12 A person the size of a thumb
Resides within the body (*ātman*)
The Lord of what was and what will be-
From him he does not hide himself.
So, indeed is that!
4.13 The person the size of a thumb
Is like a fire free of smoke;
The Lord of what was and what will be;

---

[10] The masculine form is applied until the end of the section in order to emphasize the *Paramātman* as the object, although the text uses the neuter form.

[11] 13.0. The 6th question.

[12] *BG* 13.17.

[13] Described also in *BG* 13.22.

[14] K. Klostermaier, *A Concise Encyclopedia of Hinduism* (Oxford, 1998), p. 23.

The same today and tomorrow
So, indeed is that![15]

The *Śvetāśvatara Upaniṣad*, Chapter 4, describes the relations of the two souls, the minute and the supreme as two birds nestling on the same tree:

> 6 Two birds, who are companions and friends, nestle on the very same tree. One of them eats a tasty fig; the other, not eating, looks on. 7 Stuck on the very same tree, one person grieves, deluded by her who is not the Lord. But when he sees the other, the contented Lord – and the Lord's majesty – his grief disappears.[16]

The *Paramātman* is a sort of 'personal providence' who rules, guides and accompanies the *ātman* in its journey through *saṁsāra*. As he escorts every living being separately and witnesses its deeds, he is said to possess thousands of arms and legs; as he is subtle and unseen, it is said that he is very close but at the same time hard to reach. The soul aspires to enjoy the tree's fruits or to enjoy this world and as such it experiences happiness and distress; the supreme, however, has no interest in the tree's fruits and being aloof, he merely accompanies the soul. Still, he seems to be waiting or even hoping for the soul to turn to him, although it seems that the soul is mostly occupied with the tree's fruits and mostly does not heed him. The person within the heart is a divine manifestation which encompasses both personal and impersonal traits; the *paramātman* is personal in the sense of having personal features such as a majestic form, while his impersonal aspect is expressed by his being ubiquitous. This is not to say that he is impersonal, but that his appearance in this form makes it possible for one holding an impersonal view to behold him, contemplate him, seek identity with him or even aspire to unite with him; this is in contrast to closer relationships or intense emotions which are aroused by the presence of a personal form of the divine. In concluding the section Kṛṣṇa presents an interim summary of the questions answered so far,[17] and relates this to devotion by saying that whoever is devoted to him and has acquired this knowledge can reach his nature.

Nature, the Living Entity and the Supreme Person in the Heart

> 19 Know material nature and the conscious entity to be both without beginning; know too that the transformations as well as the *guṇas* originate from material nature. 20 It is said that material nature is the cause in the matter of producing causes

---

15 Patrick Olivelle, *Upaniṣads* (Oxford, 1996), p. 242.

16 Ibid., p. 259. A similar parable appears in the *Muṇḍaka Upaniṣad*, 3.1.1–3.

17 13.18. It is to be noted that verse 18 mentions only three topics discussed, i.e. the field, knowledge and the object of knowledge. The fourth topic, i.e. the knower of the field, has been discussed too; see 13.1–2.

and effects, and that the living entity is the cause in the matter of experiencing pleasure and pain. 21 The living entity situated in material nature experiences the *guṇas* that are the product of material nature. While its association with the *guṇas* is the cause of birth in a good or bad womb. 22 The Supreme Person named *Paramātman* is said to exist in this body; he is the observing witness and the consenter, he is the supporter, he experiences everything and is the great Lord. 23 He who thus knows the living entity, the material nature and the *guṇas*, no matter what his mode of existence is, will not be reborn.

Commentary

The two remaining questions are now discussed, namely the question concerning *prakṛti* or material nature, and the question concerning the living entity or *puruṣa*. The *gunas* comprise *prakṛti*, are eternal and provide for the framework of actions and reactions, within which the living entity experiences its *karma*. The close association with the *guṇas* is the cause of *saṁsāra*; according to the interaction with the *guṇas*, the entity will take birth in a good or a bad womb. The 22nd verse adds a third and additional element to the dualism of *puruṣa* and *prakṛti*; this third element is the *Paramātman* described as *puruṣaḥ paraḥ* or the Supreme Person. He resides within the body as the witness and supporter, and at the same time shares with the minute living entity its experiences in conditioned life. This version of *Sāṅkhya* is not comprised of two, but rather is comprised of three elements: *prakṛti*, *puruṣa* and the supreme *puruṣa*, which is the supreme residing within all bodies; as such it is a theistic version of *Sāṅkhya*. This section offers a presentation of *Sāṅkhya* at its best; both *puruṣa* and *prakṛti* are described as eternal and beginningless; the *guṇas* act in the setting of *prakṛti* and cause continuous changes and endless transformations[18] in the life of every individual, as well as in the life of the entire universe. In a sense, the *guṇas* provide the general framework whereas the *puruṣa*, led by its desires, makes its way through *saṁsāra*, thus experiencing pleasure and pain.[19] The endless variety of experiences perceived by the living entity in *saṁsāra* is viewed as nothing but the experience of the three *guṇas* in various combinations; so long as the entity is engaged in experiencing the *guṇas* it remains in *saṁsāra* and takes birth in various types of wombs. The section concludes by relating this knowledge to liberation, by stating that one who understands the relations between the *puruṣa* and *prakṛti* will not be reborn.

Conclusion and Description of Various Visions

24 Some see the self by themselves through meditation and inner contemplation, others through *Sāṅkhya yoga*, while others through *Karma yoga*. 25 Still others,

[18] *Vikāra*.

[19] *BG* 6.20.

although not knowing all this, revere it upon hearing it from others. Devoted to what they have heard, they too cross beyond death. 26 O bull among the Bharatas, know that every born entity, whether still or moving, is but a combination of the field and the knower of the field. 27 He who sees the Supreme Lord, who is equally situated in all beings, not perishing when these perish, truly sees. 28 One who sees the Lord as situated equally everywhere, does not degrade himself by his mind, and thus goes to the supreme destination.[20] 29 He who sees that all activities are performed by nature alone, and that the self does not act at all, truly sees. 30 When one sees the beings' various states of existence as situated in unity, and that from that unity everything extends, he then attains *Brahman*. 31 The eternal *Paramātman*, the Supreme Person residing in the heart, although residing in the body, does nothing at all and is never tainted, because of his being without beginning and beyond the *guṇas*. 32 As ether spreads everywhere without being tainted because of its subtleness, similarly, the self abiding in every body is never tainted. 33 As the sun alone illuminates the entire universe, similarly does the owner of the field illuminates the entire field (with consciousness), O Bhārata. 34 Those, who with the eye of knowledge, can distinguish between the field and the knowner of the field, and understand the process of the entities' release from nature, will go to the Supreme.

Commentary

The chapter is summarized by evoking a wider perspective at the knowledge disclosed; four options are offered through which this knowledge can be attained:[21] meditation,[22] theoretical study,[23] *yogic* activity[24] and hearing from authorities.[25] Following this, a transition from a theoretical and rational mode of discussion to a vision or *darśana* takes place, and in verses 27–33 Kṛṣṇa endows Arjuna with various visions; this is not a presentation of a systematic thesis, rather a *darśana* or a direct experience of truths so far presented theoretically. The first vision is that of the supreme present everywhere although untainted,[26] and the second vision is concerned with the working of the *guṇas* contrasted with the passivity of the

[20] The phrase *ātmanātmānaṁ* can be understood in different ways, as the word *ātman* can be taken as 'self' in the sense of 'soul' or 'mind' and I combine the two. Although the word *hinasti* is generally translated as 'harms', 'injures' or 'hurts' I take 'degrade' to be more appropriate here.

[21] Verses 24–25.

[22] *Dhyāna*.

[23] *Sāṅkhya*.

[24] *Karma-yoga*.

[25] Apparently from a *guru* or *ṛṣi*.

[26] 13.27–28.

self.[27] The next is a vision of unity,[28] and then comes an explicit vision of the *Paramātman*.[29] The self's purity and subtleness is then compared to ether,[30] and the self is further compared to the sun, illuminating the entire universe.[31] The section's summarizing verse summarizes the chapter as well;[32] accordingly, those who see with the eyes of knowledge can distinguish between the field and the knower of the field. They understand the process by which the knower of the field can be released from the field, and it is this understanding which releases them, and enables them to attain the supreme themselves.

---

27 13.29.

28 13.30.

29 13.31.

30 13.32.

31 13.33.

32 13.34.

Chapter 14
The Three *Guṇas*

The Supreme Person, *Brahman*, Nature and the *Guṇas*

1 The blessed Lord said: Again, I shall impart unto you the highest of all wisdom, the best of knowledge, knowing which all the seers have attained supreme perfection. 2 Those resorting to this knowledge, attain a nature similar to mine; as such, they do not come to birth at the time of the cosmic creation, and are not disturbed at the time of the cosmic dissolution. 3 The great *Brahman* serves me as a womb in which I implant the seed, and thus, O Bhārata, do all living beings originate. 4 The living beings' various forms are produced in various wombs; ultimately, *Brahman* who is material nature[1] is the great womb, and I am the seed-giving father. 5 Goodness, passion and darkness are the three *guṇas* originating from the material nature; they bind the embodied eternal living entity, O mighty armed Arjuna. 6 Among these goodness, because it is untainted, illuminates and purifies, and binds one through attachment to happiness and knowledge, O sinless Arjuna. 7 Know that passion is characterized by desire; it arises from craving and attachment, and it binds the embodied soul through attachment to action, O Kaunteya. 8 Know that darkness is born of ignorance, and that it deludes all embodied souls. O Bhārata, it binds through negligence, indolence and sleep. 9 Goodness attaches one to happiness, passion attaches one to activity, O Bhārata, whereas darkness, concealing knowledge, causes attachment to heedlessness and madness.

Commentary

This chapter is engaged with the subject matter of the three *guṇas*, and as such may be taken as an elaboration or exposition of *Sāṅkhya* philosophy. Kṛṣṇa begins by stating that the knowledge he is about to introduce is of a soteriological nature; as such, it liberates from the bondage of matter, and endows one with a spiritual nature similar to his. He then proceeds to describe the origin of beings through the example of the fetus in the womb; as the soul enters the womb through the father's sperm and there develops its body, similarly, the supreme impregnates the material nature with spiritual seeds or souls, and as such, the various shapes of bodies are formed. In that sense, the Supreme Person is the father of all, whereas nature is the

---

[1] I follow Rāmānuja in equating *Brahman* with *prakṛti* or material nature; see his commentary to *BG* 14.3 in: *Śrī Rāmānuja Gītā Bhāṣya* (Madras, 1991), pp. 462–463.

mother.[2] Next, material nature or *prakṛti* comprised of the three *guṇas* is described; although the term *guṇa* is at times translated as 'quality', a deeper look will reveal that the concept of the *guṇas* is somewhat subtle, and that these are entities or substances and not mere qualities. The *guṇas* not merely characterize the subtle and gross nature of the living being, but they also actively confine it in the various types of bonds. As such, each *guṇa* binds the living entity in a particular fashion; goodness – through attachment to knowledge and happiness, passion – through attachment to activity and its fruits, and darkness – through illusion, indolence and madness. The *guṇas* not only confine, but pave a kind of an existential path for each and every individual entity; accordingly, each entity progresses in a more or less predetermined path, conforming to the *guṇas* by which it is bound. As such, it acts in a certain way, and receives consequential *karma* which keeps it bound within the same compound of *guṇas*.

The Characteristics of the *Guṇas*, and Transcending them Altogether

> 10 Goodness prevails when it overcomes passion and darkness, O Bhārata. Similarly passion prevails by overcoming goodness and darkness, and darkness – by overcoming goodness and passion. 11 When all the gates of the body are illuminated by knowledge, it is to be known that the influence of goodness increases and dominates. 12 O Bull among the Bharatas, when passion is dominant, greed, vigorous activity, venture, restlessness and yearning are born. 13 O descendant of Kuru, when darkness is dominant, obscurity, inertia, insanity and confusion are born. 14 When the embodied soul meets death influenced by goodness, it attains the pure worlds of those possessing the highest knowledge. 15 When it meets death under the influence of passion, it is reborn among those attached to activity, and when it meets death under the influence of darkness, it is reborn among the witless animals. 16 It is said that an action well performed results in a spotless fruit of the nature of goodness, but passionate action brings suffering, and action of the nature of darkness, brings with it ignorance and foolishness. 17 From goodness arises knowledge, from passion greed alone arises, and from darkness only negligence, illusion and ignorance arise. 18 Those established in goodness go upwards, those established in passion remain in the middle state, and those who are established in the lowest *guṇa* condition, in darkness, go downward. 19 When the wise one beholds no other agent performing actions save the *guṇas*, and knows that which is above the *guṇas*, he attains my state of being. 20 When the embodied soul transcends these three *guṇas* that originate in the body, it becomes liberated from birth, death, old age and misery, and attains the nectar of immortality.

---

2 14.4.

Commentary

The working of the *guṇas* is somewhat unsteady, and at different times various combinations of *guṇas* prevail. The dominance of a particular *guṇa* can be ascertained according to various symptoms; as such, when the bodily gates are controlled, apparently in a *yogic* manner, it is understood that the *guṇa* of goodness prevails. Restlessness and hankering are a symptom of the passion *guṇa*, and laziness, confusion and insanity indicate the *guṇa* of darkness's presence. One's state at the time of death is also ascertained by the *guṇas*, and accordingly the next birth is determined; goodness leads to the higher planets, passion leads to birth among those who work with a deep aspiration for the fruits of their work, and darkness leads to an animal birth, which is naturally more ignorant and obscure. A different perspective of the topic may be gained by examining action through its fruit or outcome: an action which results in a spotless result is by nature influenced by goodness, an action which results in some type of suffering is an action in passion, and an action resulting in foolishness must have been performed under the influence of the lowest *guṇa*, that of darkness. Another way of examining the *guṇas* is by saying that knowledge arises from the *guṇa* of goodness, greed arises as a result of the passion *guṇa*, and ignorance arises as a result of the darkness *guṇa*. The principle of universal progress is again confirmed by stating that those in goodness progress upwards, apparently to higher planets or higher births, those in passion remain in the middle, and those in darkness descend to lower species or lower planets. The section ends by evoking a wider vision, according to which the whole world acts under the influence of the *guṇas*, so much so that there is no other agent acting. Maintaining this vision seems to be a precondition for liberation; moreover, by transcending the *guṇas* altogether one attains liberation from birth and death and gains immortality.

What is the apparent conclusion of this discussion? It follows that the recommended course of action is within the jurisdiction of the goodness *guṇa*; also, this discussion has to do with dispelling Arjuna's doubts, as Kṛṣṇa aims at convincing Arjuna, this time through the concept of the *guṇas*, that he should take up arms and fight. Kṛṣṇa's main argument is that Arjuna's abstaining from the war is under the influence of passion and ignorance, and that he must overcome his weakness and act in the realm of goodness. Surprising as it may sound, fighting is, in Kṛṣṇa's opinion, an act of goodness, while abstaining from fighting is an action or a course of passion and ignorance. An additional point in need of clarification is the question of what is to be found beyond the *guṇas*, a point mentioned by Kṛṣṇa; this will be referred to in the coming verses, saying that *Brahman* is situated beyond the *guṇas*, and that *Brahman* rests upon Kṛṣna himself. In other words, knowledge of Kṛṣṇa is knowledge of that which is to be found beyond the *guṇas*. Arjuna seems to accept the state of liberation from the *guṇas* as being the ideal state and, as such, the next section opens with his enquiry in regards to transcending the *guṇas*.

Characteristics of One who has Transcended the *Guṇas*, *Bhakti* and the Position of the Supreme Person

> 21 Arjuna said: O Lord, by what signs is one known to have transcended these three *guṇas*? How does such a person act and how does he pass beyond them?
> 22 The Blessed Lord said: He does not despise the presence of enlightenment, activity and illusion, nor longs for them in their absence, O Pāṇḍava. 23 He is seated as if uninvolved, who is not disturbed by the *guṇas* considering that the *guṇas* alone are acting, and thus remains firm and unshaken. 24 With one mind he faces happiness and distress, grave, regarding clay, stone and gold alike, to whom pleasant and unpleasant are the same, steady and equal towards praise and blame. 25 Regarding honour and dishonour with equanimity, and similarly being the same to parties of friends and foes, renouncing every ambitious initiative, he is said to have transcended the *guṇas*. 26 And one who serves me constantly through the *yoga* of devotion (*bhakti*), unswervingly and without going astray, he transcends these *guṇas* and attains the state of *Brahman*. 27 For I am the foundation underlying *Brahman*, of the immortal, the imperishable, the eternal *dharma* and the absolute bliss.

Commentary

Kṛṣṇa presents the ideal of equanimity as characterizing the state of liberation from the *guṇas*, and describes it in detail, including the mentioning of indifference towards friends and enemies. He states that the path of *bhakti*, or devotion to himself, is the path to liberation from the bonds of the *guṇas*, leading to the spiritual level of *Brahman*; moreover, he presents himself as the foundation on which *Brahman* rests. It appears that Kṛṣṇa addresses the problem of convincing Arjuna to fight on two levels; in the first, he argues that Arjuna should fight based upon the *guṇa* concept, and in the second he encourages Arjuna to fight as an expression of devotion. The challenge facing Kṛṣṇa in the course of the first argument is to convince Arjuna solely through the concept of the *guṇas*. In this type of argument Kṛṣṇa cannot raise the argument of his divinity, rather he must establish that fighting represents goodness, and its avoidance represents passion and darkness. The challenge is not easy, but the expected argumentative gain for Kṛṣṇa is considerable, as this would strengthen the rationale underlying the entire *Bhagavad Gītā*, in that it would extend the ethical ladder all the way down to the lowest *guṇa*. Accordingly, action in passion is better than action in darkness, while action in goodness is still better; acting in goodness means adhering to one's *dharmic* duty, and this completes the formation of the ladder's lower stages and enables the construction of a complete ladder, leading all the way from the lowest *guṇa* up to *mokṣa*. In articulating the second argument, Kṛṣṇa argues that one must relinquish the world along with its three *guṇas* through *bhakti-yoga* or *yogic* devotion to Kṛṣṇa himself. The argument underlying this idea is that Kṛṣṇa is the Supreme Person and is situated above the *guṇas*, and that *Brahman* rests upon him. If Arjuna fulfils Kṛṣṇa's desire and fights, he will attain a divine nature like Kṛṣṇa's, and attain *mokṣa*. Fighting is perceived here as a practice of *bhakti yoga*, and its justification is the fact that Kṛṣṇa desires the battle for his own divine reasons.

Chapter 15
The Journey from Bondage to Liberation

The Parable of the Inverted Tree

> 1 The Blessed Lord said: it is said that there exists an eternal *Aśvattha* tree,
> whose roots are above and it's branches below; its leaves are the *Vedic* hymns,
> and its knower is the knower of the *Veda*. 2 The tree's branches, with sense
> objects as their sprouts, extend upward and downward and are nourished by the
> *guṇas*; the tree's roots which extend downward as well, are bound to activity
> in the human world. 3–4 In this world one cannot perceive the tree's form, nor
> its end, nor its origin neither its foundation; thus, this deeply rooted *Aśvattha*
> tree is to be cut down with determination by the axe of detachment. Then,
> one should search for that place, which having reached one never returns, and
> there take refuge in the Primeval Person, from whom the cosmic activity has
> emanated since time immemorial. 5 Those who are free from pride and illusion,
> who have conquered the fault of attachment and are constantly absorbed in the
> Supreme Self, whose lusts have abated, who are freed from the duality known
> as happiness and distress, not bewildered, they go to that eternal place. 6 That
> place is not illuminated by the sun or moon, nor by fire; having gone there no
> one returns. That is my Supreme abode.

Commentary

The parable of the inverted tree, knowledge of the *Vedas*, liberation from the world, searching for the Supreme Person and taking refuge in him – all these are to be found in this rich section, merely six verses long. The section begins by depicting the parable of the inverted tree – an incredibly complex tree representing the whole of material existence, or the entanglement of the soul in the world of *saṁsāra*. It is said that one who knows the *Vedas* knows or understands this complex tree; this comment is somewhat surprising in view of the various critiques of *Vedic* rituals offered earlier.[1] However, it seems that the *Vedas* are understood here in a fuller and more holistic sense, as propounding knowledge leading to liberation or as *śruti*, as opposed to rituals directed at worldly or heavenly success. The tree itself is far too complex for human understanding and as such any attempt to conceptualize or rationalize it is fruitless; therefore, one must overcome it by decisively cutting it by means of detachment. However, even this is insufficient by itself, since even after renouncing the world one must find an alternate situation or place which, having

---

1 E.g. *BG* 2.42–43.

once come to, one never returns. Such a place indeed exists and that is the abode of the Supreme Primeval Person, Śrī Kṛṣṇa. In order to stay in that supreme abode, one must establish relationship with him by seeking his shelter; this is possible only for those freed from the faults characterizing the conditioned souls such as pride and illusion. Had I been asked to summarize the entire *Bhagavad Gītā* in six verses, I would have cited this brief section, which epitomizes the whole of the treatise; the section begins with describing the deep entanglement in material existence, it then proceeds to the struggle for liberation through the cutting of the tree, while searching for an alternate location or situation, and it ends with finding that place and establishing permanent relationships with the Supreme Person.

The Soul Covered by the Senses

> 7 The eternal soul existing in this world of souls is indeed my fragment; it draws
> towards itself the six senses including the mind, which are all rooted in material
> nature. 8 When accepting a body or when relinquishing it, the prevailing soul
> carries along with it the six senses, just as air carries fragrances from their
> sources. 9 Through hearing, sight, touch, taste and smell, as well as the mind,
> it experiences the sense objects. 10 At times it remains within the body, at times
> it departs from it and at other times it takes pleasure under the *guṇas*' spell; the
> deluded cannot see all this, but rather those who possess the sight of knowledge.
> 11 The striving *yogīs* see it as situated in the self; however, the mindless who
> have not achieved self-realization, will not see this however they strive to.

Commentary

A novelty offered here is that the minute soul is but a fragment of the Supreme Person; the relations between the two seem to resemble a father and son's or daughter's relationships,[2] and this concept seems to arouse the sentiment of the father longing to reunite with his lost children. The six senses gather around the soul and accompany it in its journey through *saṁsāra*; it seems that the physical form is shaped around and based on the subtle form, as when the soul migrates from one body to another the accompanying senses shape the new body. The soul then experiences the world through the senses which perceive their objects, while the pleasure it derives from the world depends upon the *guṇas*. This vision is somewhat mystical and as such is not open to all; only self-restrained *yogīs* can attain it, whereas others, presumably those who are under the lower *guṇas*, are unable to see all this.

---

[2] See also *BG* 14.4.

The Supreme Person

12 The splendour of the sun illuminates the entire universe, and appears to be in the moon and fire as well; know that splendour to be mine. 13 Pervading the earth, I maintain the beings by my power, and becoming *Soma*,[3] whose essence is replete with taste, I nourish all plants. 14 Having become the fire of digestion abiding in the bodies of all living beings, I digest the four kinds of food with the aid of the incoming and outgoing breaths. 15 I reside in the heart of everyone; from me come memory, knowledge and reasoning. By all the *Vedas*, I alone am that which is to be known; I am also their knower and indeed, it is I who compiled the *Vedānta*. 16 There are two kinds of personalities in this world: The perishable and the imperishable; all beings are perishable, whereas that which is stable and firm is said to be imperishable.[4] 17 But there is another Person, who is the highest of all, and is called The Supreme self (*Paramātman*), who is the eternal Lord, pervading the three worlds and maintaining them. 18 Because I am beyond the perishable and transcend even the imperishable, I am renowned in the world as well as in the *Vedas* as the Supreme Person. 19 The undeluded who knows me as the Supreme Person knows all that is to be known, and devotes himself to me with his whole being, O Bhārata. 20 Thus have I revealed to you the most mysterious doctrine, O blameless Arjuna; he who has realized that, has completed his task and has become enlightened.

Commentary

This concluding section addresses rather directly Kṛṣṇa's divinity, and it no doubt comprises one of the *Bhagavad Gītā*'s peaks. It begins by describing various aspects of Kṛṣṇa's immanent divinity, including Kṛṣṇa's declaration that he is seated in everyone's heart.[5] Next Kṛṣṇa turns to the *Vedic* knowledge and states that it is actually knowledge of himself; moreover, he declares that he is the author of the *Vedānta*.[6] At the end of the section Kṛṣṇa describes the conditioned beings along with the liberated ones, and points to himself as being beyond them all, and it ends with the declaration that true knowledge indeed leads to devotion. The idea that this chapter summarizes the entire treatise is further reinforced in the concluding verse; accordingly, one who has understood these truths in regards to the soul's entanglement in the world, the process of liberation from the shackles

---

[3] *Soma* refers to both a heavenly beverage and the moon.

[4] I understand this verse in Rāmānuja's line; accordingly, the embodied souls conditioned by matter and transmigrating from body to body are the perishable. Conversely, the imperishable are the disembodied souls who attained liberation and as such have become free from the bondage of matter. See Rāmānuja, *Śrī Rāmānuja Gītā Bhāṣya* (Madras, 1991), p. 499.

[5] See the commentary on *BG* 13.12–18, pp. 106–107.

[6] *Vedānta* may refer to the *Brahmasūtras* but also to the *Upaniṣads*.

of *saṁsāra*, and the truth in regards to Śrī Kṛṣṇa's divinity, has completed his mission and has become enlightened.

Chapter 16
The Divine and the Demonic

The Two Sorts of Creatures

1 The Blessed Lord said: fearlessness, purification of one's whole being, firmness in spiritual knowledge, generosity, self-control and sacrifice, studying the *Veda*, austerity, righteousness, 2 nonviolence, truthfulness, absence of anger, renunciation, tranquillity, avoiding vilification, compassion for all beings, absence of greed, gentleness, modesty, reliability, 3 vigour, tolerance, fortitude, purity, absence of envy and pride – these are the qualities of one born to divine destiny, O Bhārata. 4 Hypocrisy, arrogance, conceit, anger, harshness and ignorance – these are the qualities of one who is born to a demonic destiny, O Pārtha. 5 The divine qualities lead to liberation whereas the demonic qualities lead to bondage; fear not, as you were born to a divine destiny. 6 In this world there are created beings[1] of two kinds – the divine and the demonic. As the divine has been extensively described, hear from me now of the demonic, O Pārtha.

Commentary

This chapter continues the discussion of human nature, a discussion begun in Chapter 13 and continued through Chapter 14. We now hear about two kinds of human beings opposed to each other – the divine and the demonic. Divine nature leads to liberation, whereas demonic nature leads to a deeper confinement in the material world. This principle has already been mentioned in Chapter 14, where the *guṇas* were depicted as kind of paths to be travelled upon by the soul in its universal journey. Accordingly, one who progresses in the path of goodness will eventually achieve liberation, and conversely, one who is bound by the opposite paths of passion and darkness, will gradually fall into lower forms of life. Since throughout the entire *Bhagavad Gītā* the qualities of the ideal person were dealt with,[2] it seems natural to deal with the demonic nature as well. A question may be raised: is the distinction between the divine and the demonic an ontological distinction? Are there actually some people who are fully demons whereas others are fully divine or at least pious? It may well be that the sharp contrast between the two kinds of beings is more of a didactic device rather than an ontological assertion or a description of reality in anthropological terms, and this may be

---

1 Literally, creations of beings.

2 E.g. *B*G 13.7–11.

asserted by considering various points. The ethical ladder, which is the central structure of the *Bhagavad Gītā*, encourages transition and ascension from step to step; according to this logic one who is destined to a certain fate or to demonic nature can also climb the ladder and purify his existence. This principle is further reinforced at the end of Chapter 9, where it is stated that even those born of lowly origin can attain the supreme destination.[3] The apparent association between the divine nature and the *guṇa* of goodness, and between the demonic nature and the *guṇas* of passion and darkness, raises the assumption that the ethical ladder extends in one continuum from the lowest point, namely the *guṇa* of darkness, all the way up to the highest point which is liberation from the world. It was already mentioned in Chapter 14 that the *guṇas* compete among themselves,[4] so it seems that there is no position of pure goodness, nor one of passion and darkness entirely devoid of goodness, rather every combination is a mixture of various proportions. Also, in the broader epic context of the *Bhagavad Gītā*, the *Mahābhārata*, it is apparent that no figure is entirely pure, and that demons, too, have positive traits. Considering all these points it may well be that the sharp distinction between the divine and the demonic is more didactic than ontological.

The Demons' World

> 7 Demonic people do not know when to act and when to avoid acting; not purity,
> nor proper conduct nor truth is to be found in them. 8 They claim that this world
> is unreal, lacking a solid foundation, not controlled by the supreme, and that
> it originates not from causal succession but rather that lust alone is its cause. 9
> Maintaining such a view, these lost souls of little intelligence, enemies to all,
> initiate horrible acts aiming to destroy the world. 10 Resorting to insatiable lust,
> filled with hypocrisy, pride and intoxication and accepting false ideas out of
> illusion, they proceed with their impure way of life. 11 Subject to boundless
> anxiety ending with death only, they are convinced that there is nothing higher
> than gratification of desires. 12 Being trapped and bound by hundreds of hopes,
> absorbed in desire and anger, they seek to accumulate wealth by improper means
> in order to indulge in their lusts. 13 'This much have I accumulated today, and
> that wish shall I obtain later on. This wealth is already mine whereas that wealth
> will become mine. 14 I have slain that enemy and the others will similarly be
> slain; I am the lord, I am the enjoyer, perfect I am, powerful and happy! 15 I am
> wealthy and of a high family; who else equals me? I shall sacrifice, give charity
> and rejoice'. This is the mind and view of those whom ignorance bewilders.
> 16 Led astray by a multitude of thoughts, captured in the net of delusion and
> addicted to enjoying lusty desires, they fall into the abominable hell. 17 Self-

---

3 *BG* 9.32.

4 *BG* 14.10.

centred and stubborn, arrogant and wealth-intoxicated, hypocritically they offer sacrifices in name only without following proper scriptural injunctions.

Commentary

This section is sharply critical of the demons, and highlights the basic assumptions underlying the demonic world view: accordingly this world is unreal and lacks a solid foundation, is not controlled by the supreme and emerges out of lust alone.[5] Who is the text arguing with, or stated differently, who holds and spreads such tenets? It may well be that the *Cārvākas* are those for whom there is no question of any divine power in control, the text may be possibly hinting at the *mīmāṁsakas* for whom it is somewhat irrelevant whether the world is controlled by the supreme or not, and it may also hint at the Buddhists, who consider the world to be in a sense unreal. The psychological analysis is penetrating and well phrased; the personality of the demonic person who is full of longings and desires, is depicted most critically, indicating the tangle of fears he is subjected to due to his endless desires. The perpetual effort for self-glorification, an effort designed to hide the absurd condition of one who maintains his own superiority, is well described.[6] The criticism also addresses false religiosity and hypocrisy, in the name of which the demonic person performs sacrifices and charity; as such this section furnishes a brief but profound analysis of the demonic personality. Could this description be intended to cause Arjuna to reflect whether any of this refers to him too? Possibly this section may also have its role in Arjuna's process of purification, by turning his attention inside and allowing him to deeply reflect upon his tenets and inner convictions.

The Supreme Person's Relations with the Demons

18 Influenced by egotism, aggressiveness, insolence, lust and anger, these envious
people hate me, who am present in their own bodies as well as in the bodies of
others. 19 I ceaselessly cast down those hateful, cruel, wretched and inauspicious
people into demonic wombs, deeper into the cycle of birth and death. 20 Having
entered demonic wombs birth after birth, these deluded people do not attain me,
Kaunteya, hence they proceed to the worst destination. 21 Lust, anger and greed
are the three gates of hell and the destroyers of the self; they should therefore be
abandoned. 22 O Kaunteya, one who is freed from these three gates to darkness
acts for the benefit of the self, and thus proceeds to the highest destination. 23
He who ignores scriptural injunctions and follows his own lustful whims, attains
not perfection, nor happiness nor the supreme destination. 24 Therefore, let the

5 16.8.

6 16.13–15.

> *śāstra*[7] guide you in discriminating between what is to be done and what is not to be done; knowing what the scriptures enjoin, you should adhere to your duty.

Commentary

The section looks at the interaction between the Supreme Person and the demonic person; the latter hates the Supreme Person, who in turn throws him further into *saṁsāra*. Lust, anger and greed are portrayed as gates to hell, and Arjuna is advised to abandon them altogether. Kṛṣṇa then suggests to Arjuna the *śāstra* as means of discrimination between the demonic and the divine paths. Taking a wider perspective, this chapter undoubtedly makes a significant contribution to the discussion of human nature by dealing with the hitherto scarcely discussed demonic way of life. Also, the occupation with one of the central topics raised in the *Bhagavad Gītā* – the topic of evil and the subsequent fall to lower forms of existence deserves mention. Previously, Arjuna had argued against fighting, declaring that those who destroy the dynasty will dwell in hell, being immersed in evil.[8] In the present chapter Kṛṣṇa further confronts the question by presenting two kinds of persons taking two different routes: the divine who follow the scriptural decrees and are thus progressing towards liberation, as opposed to the demonic, who act according to the follies of their hearts, who averse the Supreme Person, and as such progress towards hell. Kṛṣṇa considers Arjuna to belong to the first group and as such he should follow the scriptures by adhering to his duty and fight; in this way he will be avoiding the demonic destination.

---

7 Scriptures.

8 *BG* 1.43–44.

Chapter 17
The Manifestation of the Three *Guṇas* in Human Life

One's Essential Nature is His Faith

1 Arjuna said: O Kṛṣṇa, those who have cast aside the scriptural injunctions, yet
are imbued with faith and still sacrifice, what is their position? Is it in goodness,
passion or darkness? 2 The blessed Lord said: embodied souls have three kinds
of faith originating from their nature, and these are goodness, passion and
darkness; hear then of them. 3 O Bhārata, one's faith is according to his essential
nature, as the human being is composed of faith; indeed, whatever his faith is
– that's what he is.

Commentary

The question of liberation has been dealt with, and it appears that Arjuna accepts that liberation can be attained through following the scriptures and rising above the *guṇas*. Now he enquires in regards to the condition of those who do not follow the scriptures, and apparently are not established on the path leading to liberation. They still function in the world in various ways, offer some sacrifices, eat this or that food, donate to charity, etc., and as such, he enquires as to their existential state. Kṛṣṇa begins his reply by evoking the higher vision of the body and soul,[1] and says that embodied souls are bound by the *guṇas* or are rather conditioned by them. The third verse outlines the discussion's scope; one's essential nature is his faith, which is characterized by the *guṇas* alone; it seems that the word 'faith' here does not refer to a religious faith in the supreme, rather it refers to one's tastes or rather inclinations, representing his nature, or his constitution of the *guṇas*, and as such, the following discussion is confined within the boundaries of the *guṇas*. Stated differently, it is a discussion of human nature considered from a more worldly point of view;[2] i.e. without consideration of the metaphysical duality between the body and soul, without consideration of any relations to the Supreme Person, and without consideration of liberation.

---

1 The 'second tier' vision.

2 I.e. the 'first tier' vision.

Worship, Demonic Austerity and Food

4 Persons of goodness worship the gods, persons of passion worship *yakṣas* and *rākṣasas*[3] whereas those of darkness worship ghosts and spirits. 5 The hearts of those who practice dreadful austerities not ordained by the scriptures, are filled with hypocrisy and egotism as they are motivated by lust and attachment. 6 Those fools, who torture the aggregate of elements in their bodies as well as me, who dwell therein, know them to have a demonic resolution. 7 Moreover, the food that all do like is of three kinds, and similarly divided are sacrifice, austerity and charity; hear too of these. 8 Food preferred by persons of goodness increases lifespan, strength, health, happiness and satisfaction; it is tasty, mild, substantial and pleasant to the heart. 9 Food desired by men of passion is pungent, sour, salty, too hot and dry – scorching and burning and causes suffering, misery and disease. 10 Food dear to persons of darkness is stale, tasteless and putrid, consisting of leftovers and abominations.

Commentary

A more detailed discussion of the *guṇas* and their expressions in various aspects of human life now commences; apparently religious practice is not necessarily always beyond the *guṇas* and as such worship is divided according to the three *guṇas*.

Next, austerities are examined and it follows that not every austerity undertaken is in goodness, rather there are austerities in passion and darkness as well. The criticism of asceticism may also hint at Arjuna who has considered forsaking the battle, abandoning his *dharmic* duty as a warrior, and turning into an ascetic. This is so since various severe austerities are taken to be demonic and not necessarily in goodness or spiritual. The subject of food provides a basic measure for characterizing human nature according to the *guṇas*, since everyone eats some kind of food. According to the *guṇa* concept, food of the nature of goodness is composed of vegetables, beans, fresh milk, and fruits; food in passion is also vegetarian but is spicy and less delicate, such as fried foods, sorts of cheese and mixed nuts, whereas food categorized as dark is composed of meat, fish, eggs and alcoholic drinks.

Sacrifice, Austerity and Charity

11 Sacrifice offered without interest in its fruits, performed according to scripture and out of a deep sense of duty and conviction that it should be performed, is of the nature of goodness. 12 But the sacrifice performed with its fruits in mind, out of hypocrisy and for the purpose of ostentation, know that sacrifice to be of the

[3] Types of demons.

nature of passion, O best of the Bhāratas. 13 The sacrifice performed in neglect of scriptural injunctions, without distributing food, without the chanting of mantras or donations to the brahmins, and without faith is said to be of the nature of darkness. 14 Worship of the gods, of brahmins, of teachers and wise men as well as purity, honesty, celibacy and nonviolence, are said to be the austerity of the body. 15 Words that do not agitate others, and are truthful, pleasant and beneficial, as well as constant recitation of scriptures are said to be the austerity of speech. 16 Peace of mind, gentleness, silence, self-control and purification of one's existence are said to be the austerity of the mind. 17 This threefold austerity is said to be of the nature of goodness when performed with deep faith by persons disciplined through *yoga*, expecting no fruit in return. 18 Austerity is said to be of the nature of passion when hypocritically performed for the sake of winning reverence, honour and distinction; it is ephemeral and unstable. 19 Austerity is said to be of the nature of darkness when performed out of obscure notions and self-torture, or with the aim of harming others. 20 Charity is held to be of the nature of goodness when the gift is bestowed upon one who has not performed a prior service, with a sense of duty and conviction that it ought to be given, and when offered at the proper place, at the proper time and to a worthy person. 21 But when charity is given in expectation of some gain, with its fruits in mind or offered grudgingly, that gift is considered to be of the nature of passion. 22 That charity given at the wrong time and place, to an unworthy person, without paying respect and with contempt is said to be of the nature of darkness.

Commentary

Kṛṣṇa now emphasizes the *guṇas*' internal aspects as opposed to the external ones underlying their initial description. Previously the description given was that goodness is serene, passion is active and darkness is drowsy; now the description emphasizes the inner attitude of the agent performing action rather than the external characters mentioned. The question ceases to be whether one should offer sacrifices, undergo austerities or give charity, but instead – how should these acts be performed internally, and in what mood; phrased differently, the question now raised is 'by what motive should action be performed'. Initially, Kṛṣṇa has spoken of the *guṇas* out of a world-renouncing attitude, describing the world of the *guṇas* as characterizing *saṁsāra* and hence to be renounced; here he takes a different approach and utilizes the discussion of the *guṇas* to call for internalization. As such, each and every action can possibly be performed in three different ways; in goodness, in passion and in darkness. Each mode of action has its implications and the conclusion is that acting in goodness is the recommended course. The logic seems clear: fighting in goodness will be in accordance with *dharma*, out of duty and performed for its own sake; fighting in passion will be with the aim of gaining fruits such as honour or success, and fighting in a state of darkness will be in the wrong time and place, against the wrong enemy and out of illusion. The list describing the austerities of body, speech and mind reminds one of the Patañjali's *yoga-sūtra*, in which the *yogī* practices celibacy, scriptural study and speaking the truth.[4]

Oṁ, Tat, Sat

> 23 The threefold expression *Oṁ Tat Sat* indicates *Brahman*. It has been used since the days of yore to ordain the brahmins, the *Vedas* and sacrifices. 24
> Therefore, acts of sacrifice, charity and austerity undertaken by those aspiring for *Brahman*, are initiated by the chanting of *Oṁ* as tradition ordains. 25 The
> phrase *Tat* initiates various acts of sacrifice, austerity and charity performed by those desirous of liberation, who have no interest in the fruits of these acts. 26 *Sat*
> is used to indicate the 'real', as well as the 'good'. Thus the word *Sat* is used as regards every praiseworthy action, O Pārtha. 27 Also, steadfastness in the matter of sacrifice, austerity and charity is called *Sat*; every action with this aim is also called *Sat*. 28 When performed without faith, offering of an oblation, giving of a gift and practicing austerity are called *Asat*:[5] they have no value in this world, nor in the next, O Pārtha.

Commentary

Having discussed sacrifice, charity and austerity from the viewpoint of the *guṇas*, the present section connects these three types of activities to the absolute level. As such, the deeper meaning of these three types of activities is a search for liberation and an attempt to reach *Brahman*. Therefore, the performance of sacrifice, charity and austerity is preceded by the words *Oṁ*, *Tat* and *Sat*.

---

4 See: *Yogasūtra of Patañjali*, 2.29–32.

5 Unreal.

Chapter 18
Summary and Conclusion: Taking Refuge in Kṛṣṇa Alone

Distinguishing *Sannyāsa* from Renunciation

1 Arjuna said: O mighty armed Hṛṣīkeśa, I wish to know the meaning of *sannyāsa*, the meaning of renunciation (*tyāga*), and the difference between them.[1] 2 The Blessed Lord said: Relinquishing actions motivated by desire is known by sages as *sannyāsa*, whereas relinquishing the fruits of all actions, seers declare to be renunciation. 3 Some wise men maintain that all actions should be abandoned, since they are inherently faulty, whereas others maintain that actions of sacrifice, giving and austerity should not be abandoned. 4 O Best of the Bhāratas, hear now my decisive opinion in the matter of renunciation; O Arjuna, renunciation is declared to be of three kinds. 5 Acts of sacrifice, giving and austerity are not to be given up, but rather should be performed, as sacrifice, giving and austerity purify even the wise.

Commentary

Arjuna has previously asked whether action should be adhered to or relinquished in favour of enlightenment, and Kṛṣṇa has recommended the course of enlightened or *yogic* action.[2] The subject matter is certainly complex as Kṛṣṇa seems to not only denote the term *yogic action*,[3] but to propound both renunciation and action, terms which seem to stand in contrast to each other. Arjuna now deepens the question, asking for a clear differentiation between the order of *sannyāsa* and renunciation, the implication being that the dichotomy is not between the path of knowledge and the path of action, rather between the renunciation of action altogether and the mere renunciation of its fruits. The direction emerging is that the order of *sannyāsa* represents the relinquishment of action altogether, whereas renunciation (*tyāga*) represents the mere renunciation of action's fruits. Kṛṣṇa intends to employ the doctrine of the *guṇas*, and to recommend the course of action in goodness as a pure or renounced mode of action. He seems to apply the

---

[1] The terms *sannyāsa* and *tyāga* are not only similar but both could be translated in various ways. Based on the text itself, I am keeping the term *sannyāsa* without change, taking it to mean the fourth social order (*āśrama*), and translate the term *tyāga* as renunciation.

[2] *BG* 3.1–8, 5.1–6.

[3] *Karma yoga.*

term 'actions motivated by desire' in order to differentiate the *sannyāsa āśrama* from the *gṛhastha āśrama*; accordingly the latter is motivated by desire whereas the former lacks such a motivation. The householder performs various activities, underlain by a desire for worldly life; as such he acts for the maintenance of the family and the society, performs sacrifices with the aim of achieving prosperity and the fulfilment of desires in this world and the next. On the contrary, the *sannyāsin* relinquishes all such actions and performs only actions aiming at liberation, such as the study of the scriptures or the performance of different austerities. Having said that, Kṛṣṇa acknowledges the controversy concerning the relinquishment of action: one approach argues that the course of action should be abandoned altogether, due to its inherent faults; apparently, according to this view *sannyāsa* or renunciation is required in order to achieve liberation. This view is repeatedly raised by Arjuna, considering the option of fighting to be aiming at personal happiness at the expense of others, and therefore tainted by selfishness.[4] The alternative approach maintains that one should adhere to sacrifice, charity and asceticism, which are all discussed in the previous chapter. Kṛṣṇa supports this position and says that these actions purify even the wise; as such, he ascribes the quality of purification to action and hence it becomes *yogic action*.[5] It seems that the faults inherent in action are accepted, and in order to overcome these faults, one should perform action as a sacrifice, charity or austerity. This performance will result in self-purification and that will elevate the agent higher and higher on the 'ethical ladder'. As such, instead of becoming a degrading force, entangling one deeper and deeper in *saṁsāra*, when rightly performed in the mode of goodness, action can and should elevate one just like the performance of sacrifice, the giving of charity and the practice of austerity.

The topic of sacrifice, charity and austerity has already been discussed in the previous chapter.[6] Accordingly, sacrifice is of the nature of goodness when 'performed according to scriptural injunctions, and out of a deep sense of duty and conviction that the sacrifice ought to be performed'.[7] Austerity is of the nature of goodness when 'performed with deep faith by persons disciplined through *yoga*',[8] and charity is held to be of the nature of goodness when 'the gift is bestowed upon him who has not performed a prior service, with a sense of duty and conviction that it ought to be given'.[9] These three are performed according to scriptural injunctions, with a conviction that they ought to be performed with faith and discipline, and with a deep sense of duty. As such, it seems that the performance of sacrifice, austerity and charity, performed in the mode of goodness, is identical with adhering to *dharma* in a deep and essential sense. This identification between

---

4 E.g. *BG* 1.45.

5 There is a direct link between *yoga* and purification – e.g. *BG* 6.12.

6 *BG* 17.11–22.

7 *BG* 17.11.

8 *BG* 17.17.

9 *BG* 17.20.

the *guṇa* of goodness and *dharma* is one of the foundations of the *Bhagavad Gītā*'s structure; it connects the framework of *dharma* with the metaphysics of *Sāṅkhya* and *Yoga*, and creates one unified and solid structure which covers every sphere of human life, leading to release from *saṁsāra*. The underlying logic is that it is better to perform an action in the mode of passion than in the mode of darkness, and an action in the mode of goodness is preferable to action in the mode of passion. Acting in the mode of goodness is identical with adhering to *dharma* for its own sake, and from this position it is recommended to progress further and rise to the stage of action for the sake of the highest good, action as a practice of *yoga*, and ultimately action as a direct loving service to the Supreme Person.

The Different Kinds of Renunciation

> 6 My final judgment, Pārtha, is that these actions should be performed out of duty, abandoning attachment and interest in their fruits. 7 One's prescribed duty should not be renounced; when one renounces his duty out of delusion, that renunciation is to be considered of the nature of darkness. 8 When one renounces his duty for fear of bodily difficulties, thinking it too troublesome, his renunciation is considered to be of the nature of passion, and thus he does not reap the fruit of his renunciation. 9 When one performs his prescribed duty having abandoned any attachment and desire for fruits whatsoever, considering only that it ought to be done, his renunciation is of the nature of goodness, O Arjuna. 10 He whose renunciation is of the nature of goodness, is a wise person whose doubts have been destroyed; he does not reject undesired action, and is not attached to desired action. 11 An embodied soul is not able to completely give up activity, but he who renounces action's fruits is said to have truly renounced. 12 For him who has not renounced, actions bear three kinds of fruits to be met after death; the undesired, the desired and the mixed. However, for him who has actually renounced, there are no such fruits whatsoever.

Commentary

The present section deepens the relationship between the institution of *dharma* and the *guṇas*; accordingly, *dharma* is supported by the doctrine of the *guṇas* in that it represents the state of goodness. Kṛṣṇa has clearly expressed his opinion that one must perform actions of sacrifice, charity and austerity, actions that represent the core of *dharma*; these actions are to be performed out of duty, which is the prime driving force for the human being within the framework of the *dharma* institution. Three approaches in regards to carrying out *dharma* are articulated, and these are in accordance with the three *gunas*; non-performance of duty due to illusion is in the mode of darkness, non-performance of duty due to fear of suffering is in the mode of passion and the performance of duty for its own sake – without interest in its fruits – this is in the mode of goodness. Kṛṣṇa repeats an argument mentioned before, according to which activity is forced upon the embodied.[10] The underlying logic is clear; as it is not possible to cease from acting, the question is not whether one should act or refrain from action, but rather in what mode one should act; in darkness, passion or goodness. Apparently, acting in the mode of goodness represents the proper and desirable attitude towards renunciation. The subject matter of *karma* is raised, by speaking of the fruits to be encountered after death by one who is not renounced; these are the desirable, the undesirable and the mixed. This point invites discussion of the question whether goodness binds as well; although it has been previously stated that goodness binds one to happiness and knowledge,[11] it seems that according to the present section, action in goodness, without attachment to the deed or its fruits, does not bind one to its reactions. As such, if one acts in goodness, solely out of duty, indifferent to the deed itself, having no interest in its fruits, he will be considered renounced in this life as well as in the life to come, and will not suffer reactions to his deeds. This section also answers Arjuna who has previously claimed that fighting will make him suffer reactions and send him to hell in his next life.[12] The reply given is that Arjuna must adhere to his duty of fighting in the mode of goodness; as such, he should fight for the sake of fighting, out of duty and without interest in the fighting's fruits. Relinquishment of fighting in order to avoid possible suffering represents the mode of passion, and will result in corresponding fruits in this and the next life. Forsaking the battle out of the illusion regarding the death of the eternal soul along with the body, is a form of ignorance which represents the *guṇa* of darkness. Kṛṣṇa will now elaborate on the linkage between one's personal interest in the fruits of the deed, and the reactions which may ensue following the performance of that deed, through discussing the five causes for action.

The Five Causes for a Successful Action

> 13 O mighty armed Arjuna, learn from me of the five causes described in *Sāṅkhya*, for the successful accomplishment of all actions. 14 These are the body comprising the basis for action, the agent, the various organs of action, the types of endeavour, and providence. 15 Whatever action one performs with body, speech or mind, whether proper and right or improper and wrong, is caused by these five factors. 16 That being so, he who due to incomplete understanding sees himself as the sole agent, is a fool who does not actually see. 17 He who is not conditioned by a false conception of the self as the doer, and whose intelligence is not tainted, even though he may slay these men, does not actually kill and is not bound by this action.

---

[10] *BG* 18.11 and 3.5.

[11] *BG* 14.6.

[12] *BG* 1.44.

Commentary

Five factors underlie action; the first being the agent and the other four being external; these are the body, the various organs of action, the various types of endeavour and providence. It seems that the agent is taken to be the soul and, as such, is different from the body, from the organs, from the endeavour and of course from providence. As such, one who considers himself to be the sole doer is under illusion, whereas one who is not under such an illusion, does not kill even if he fights and kills. How is that so? It seems that the agent is not responsible for the four factors as these are all external and not under his direct control;[13] this leaves the responsibility only as far as the fifth factor or the agent himself. However, it has just been stated that if the performer of the deed has renounced his action's fruits, he will not experience good, bad or mixed reactions in his next life.[14] This renunciation is based on knowledge, as in order to be deeply renounced, one has to give up his false identity with the body and mind, consider himself a non-material soul, and realize that he has nothing to do with the various subtle and gross sense objects. Hence, the conclusion is that 'he who is not conditioned by a false conception of the self as the doer, and whose intelligence is not tainted, even though he may slay these men, does not actually kill and is not bound by this action'.[15] The argument is approximately this: you, Arjuna, are deliberating whether to fight or decline from the war, since you believe that the result of your decision will affect reality. Actually you are wrong, since you really don't govern your actions as you think you do; there are five factors, four of which are external to yourself, and only one is essentially yourself. As far as the four, you are not really responsible and only the fifth involves yourself directly. Regarding the fifth, which is the agent or yourself, you should act in the right way, maintain the proper understanding of action and disregard the action's fruits. As your action will be motivated by adherence to duty alone, and as it will be performed in the mode of goodness, you shall not be agitating the *guṇas*, will not actually kill anyone and naturally not suffer any kind of reaction. Stated differently, by acting in a pure way, with full knowledge, detachment and a sense of duty, Arjuna will be adhering to *dharma* and even his killing will not entangle him in any kind of *karmic* reaction.[16] These ideas may only be accepted assuming the soul to be eternal and entirely separated from the body. Only from such a detached position may Arjuna observe both himself and the various warriors as embodied souls, while introspectively examining himself, his attachments and his subtle motivations.

13 One may argue that the body, the organs and the endeavour are controlled by oneself, or at least represent one's *karma*, but it seems that the underlying logic here is that the soul is radically different from these three and in that sense there is no direct linkage between them.

14 *BG* 18.12.

15 *BG* 18.17.

16 See also *BG* 4.16–22.

Three Sorts of Knowledge, Actions and Agents

> 18 Knowledge, the object of knowledge and the knower are the three incentives
> motivating action. The instrument, the act and the agent are the three components
> of action. 19 Knowledge, action and the agent are indeed of three kinds, divided
> according to the *guṇas*; hear now how is this division depicted through the *guṇa*
> doctrine. 20 Know that knowledge to be of the nature of goodness, through which
> one sees a single imperishable reality in all beings, unified in the diversified. 21
> Know that knowledge to be of the nature of passion, through which one sees
> through division a variegated reality of many sorts in all beings. 22 Knowledge
> that attaches one to one kind of activity, as if it were all, which is not based on
> a reasonable cause, which does not aim at the truth, and which is minute and
> meagre, is said to be of the nature of darkness. 23 It is said that an action is of
> the nature of goodness when performed according to the injunctions of *dharma*,
> without attachment, devoid of attraction or repulsion, by one who desires not its
> fruits. 24 But action performed to satisfy one's own desires, accomplished by great
> effort or accompanied by an exaggerated ego notion, is said to be of the nature of
> passion. 25 An action performed without considering future consequences, loss
> or injury to others, disregarding one's ability to accomplish it, and undertaken
> out of delusion, is said to be of the nature of darkness. 26 An agent is said to be
> of the nature of goodness when he is free from attachment and self-absorption,
> determined, courageous and enthusiastic, and unchanged in success or failure. 27
> An agent is considered to be of passionate nature when he is passionate, covets
> the fruits of his actions, greedy, harmful, impure and absorbed in joy and sorrow.
> 28 He who is undisciplined, vulgar, stubborn, crooked, vile, indolent, dejected
> and procrastinating, such an agent is said to be of the nature of darkness.

Commentary

This section addresses, yet again, the core question of the *Bhagavad Gīta*; what is better – knowledge or action? Seen from the *guṇas*' point of view, there really is no real dichotomy between knowledge and action, rather the two are complementary. Both knowledge and action can be practiced in the mode of goodness, passion or ignorance. As such, knowledge, action and the agent are all divided into three categories according to the three *guṇas*, and the recommended path is to live in the sphere of goodness, while avoiding the spheres of passion and darkness. The agent living within the sphere of goodness is free from attachment and self-absorption, is determined, courageous and maintains a steady enthusiasm in both success and failure. His knowledge is such that he sees unity in diversity, or a single imperishable reality in all beings. His mode of action is according to the injunctions of *dharma*, without attachment, above sensual attraction or repulsion, and devoid of a desire for his actions' fruits. The agent living within the sphere of passion is greedy for his action's fruits, harmful, passionate, impure and affected by joy and sorrow. His knowledge is such that he sees reality as divided in variegated ways. His actions are performed with the aim of satisfying his desires, and are accompanied by a great effort and an exaggerated sense of ego. The agent living within the sphere of darkness is undisciplined, vulgar, stubborn, indolent, dejected and procrastinating; his knowledge is minute and meagre, is not based upon a reasonable cause and doesn't aim at the truth. He performs actions without consideration of future consequences, loss or injury to others, and disregards his ability to accomplish them. In a sense, the direction developed throughout the entire *Bhagavad Gītā* has been concluded; the dichotomy between knowledge and action was replaced by a new dichotomy, between the higher mode of action which is in goodness, and lower mode of action enacted within the sphere of passion and darkness. That accomplished, the ethical ladder is now completed; knowledge and action are now intertwined. As such, one who possesses the right understanding or has the right knowledge, acts in the mode of goodness, according to *dharma* and without regards to the fruits of action. This mode of action comprises the foundation for a deeper, *Upaniṣadic* type of understanding, according to which various spiritual truths are revealed through the performance of duty, articulated schematically through the 'ethical ladder'.

Intelligence, Determination, Happiness and the Four Social Classes

> 29 Intelligence and determination are both divided according to the three *guṇas*;
> hear now a complete detailed explanation, O Dhanañjaya. 30 The intelligence
> that discriminates between active involvement and inactive extinction, between
> what is duty and what is not, between what is to be feared and what is not to be
> feared, between what binds and what liberates, is of the nature of goodness. 31
> The intelligence that fails to distinguish between *dharma* and *adharma*,[17] and
> between what should be done and what should not, is of the nature of passion.
> 32 That obscure intelligence which takes *adharma* for *dharma*, and perceives
> all things in a perverted fashion, is of the nature of darkness, O Pārtha. 33 The
> determination that sustains the functions of the mind, life air and the senses
> through a firm practice of *yoga*, is of the nature of goodness, O Pārtha. 34 The
> determination that adheres to *dharma*, *kāma* and *artha*,[18] O Arjuna, motivated by
> attachment and a desire for the fruits, is of the nature of passion, O Pārtha. 35 The
> determination with which a dull-witted person refuses to relinquish sleep, fear,
> sorrow, dejection and intoxication, is of the nature of darkness, O Pārtha. 36 O
> Bull among the Bharatas, hear from me now of the three kinds of happiness; that
> which following a constant practice yields joy as well as the end of suffering, 37
> that which starts just like poison, but is gradually transformed to resemble nectar,
> that which springs from the tranquillity of one's heart and soul, that happiness
> is said to be of the nature of goodness. 38 The happiness emanating from contact

---

[17] *Adharma*: that which is contrary to *dharma*.

[18] *Kāma*: fulfillment of desires; *artha*: worldly success.

of the senses with their objects, which begins just like nectar, but is gradually transformed to resemble poison, is known to be of the nature of passion. 39 The happiness that deludes the self from beginning to end, and arises from sleep, indolence and negligence, is said to be of the nature of darkness. 40 There is no being neither on earth, nor among the gods in heaven, free from these three *guṇas* born of material nature. 41 O Parantapa, the activities of *brāhmaṇas*,[19] *kṣatriyas*, *vaiśyas* and *śūdras* are divided according to the *guṇas* and spring from their own nature. 42 Tranquillity, self-restraint, austerity, purity, tolerance, honesty, knowledge, wisdom and religious piety characterize the *brāhmaṇa* as they spring from his own nature. 43 Heroism, ardour, determination, expertise, fighting spirit, generosity and leadership characterize the *kṣatriya* as they spring from his own nature. 44 Agriculture, cow protection and trade characterize the *vaiśya* as they spring from his own nature, and acts of service mark the *śūdra* as they spring from his own nature.

Commentary

Intelligence within the sphere of goodness serves the purpose of liberation from *saṁsāra*; as such, it discriminates between worldly involvement and its opposite or the extinction of worldly affairs. Similarly, it discriminates between that which is to be feared from, i.e. *saṁsāra*, and that which is not to be feared from, i.e. that which leads to liberation, and it also discriminates between duty according to *dharma*, and that which exists outside the framework of *dharma*. Intelligence within the sphere of passion finds it difficult to discriminate between *dharma* and *adharma*, and intelligence within the sphere of darkness perceives reality in a perverted way, thus taking *dharma* to be *adharma* and vice versa. Determination which sustains one's psycho-physical functions through a firm *yoga* practice is considered to be in goodness. The determination required to achieve the three aims of life – *dharma*, *kāma* and *artha* for the purpose of enjoyment is considered to be in passion, whereas the determination which cannot go beyond sleep, fear, sorrow, depression and intoxication is considered to be in darkness. Although happiness in goodness begins with some suffering due to the burden of practice, that practice gradually becomes more gratifying, and is ultimately transformed into deep happiness. Happiness in passion is fundamentally different, and is based upon immediate sensual and mental satisfaction which is later transformed into suffering. Happiness in darkness is characterized by illusion from beginning to end, and is based upon the pleasure derived from indolence, sleep and negligence. This section concludes the discussion of the *guṇas*, by establishing a clear connection between the *guṇas* and the social structure underlying the institution of *dharma*. The four social classes are defined according to the *guṇas* dominating their nature; the *brahmins* are dominated by goodness, the *kṣatriyas* are dominated by a greater amount of passion, the *vaiśyas* by a lower mixture of the *guṇas*, apparently by

[19] Sanskrit: *Brāhmaṇa*. English: Brahmin.

passion and darkness, and *śūdras* are dominated predominantly by a still lower mixture of the *guṇas*. It seems that the underlying logic is that each of these groups functions in a different realm of consciousness; the *brahmins* contemplate *Brahman* or the highest truth, the *kṣatriyas* are adept at leading the masses and controlling them by political and military means, the *vaiśyas* are oriented towards raising domestic animals and crops and trading with these, while the *śūdras*' horizon is even more limited, and as such service under direction of others suits their nature the most. The section ends with the declaration that the *guṇas* are all-pervading; this highlights the importance of the *guṇa* concept and turns it into a universal, all-encompassing philosophy.

The Ethical Ladder of Values – a Summary

> 45 Being inspired to perform his own *dharmic* duty, one attains perfection; hear now how he becomes successful through contentment in following his own duty. 46 By worshiping through adhering to his own duty, him from whom all beings have originated and by whom this whole universe is pervaded, one reaches perfection. 47 Better to perform one's own duty imperfectly than another's *dharma* perfectly, as when one performs the duties prescribed for his own nature, he incurs no evil. 48 Although action is by nature deficient, it should nevertheless not be relinquished, as fault accompanies every enterprise even as smoke covers fire. 49 He whose intelligence is unattached in all respects, who has conquered himself and whose desires are gone, attains the highest perfection of actionlessness through renunciation. 50 O Kaunteya, having attained perfection, learn from me in brief how he also attains *Brahman*, the supreme state of knowledge. 51 Absorbed in the highest reality with the help of his purified intellect, restraining himself with determination, having relinquished the sense objects such as sound and others, and casting aside attraction and repulsion alike, 52 residing in solitude, eating lightly, restraining his speech, body and mind, constantly absorbed in meditation, taking refuge in dispassion, 53 freed from egotism, aggressiveness, pride, lust, anger and acquisitiveness, considering nothing to be his own and quite at peace, he becomes fit for *Brahman* realization. 54 When his whole being becomes one with *Brahman* he is pervaded by a deep peace, he grieves not nor does he crave, he becomes impartial to all creatures, and attains supreme devotion unto me. 55 Through devotion he comes to know me as I truly am; having actually realized me, he immediately attains me. 56 Although always engaged in various activities, taking refuge in me he attains by my grace the eternal and imperishable abode.

Commentary

The discussion has ended and now Kṛṣṇa begins to summarize the entire *Bhagavad Gītā*; the present section highlights the *Bhagavad Gītā*'s structure – the ethical ladder intertwined with the three tiers of reality. This section first summarizes the philosophy of action representing the first tier,[20] it then summarizes the stage of *yogic* detachment representing the second tier,[21] and at last, summarizes the ladder's highest stage of attaining *Brahman* representing the third tier.[22] The philosophy of action presented in a nutshell is a summary of topics discussed in various sections of the *Bhagavad Gītā*, and especially Chapters 3 and 5 and, as such, verse 47 of the present section is a paraphrase of verse 3.35. The state of detachment from worldly existence and the development of attachment towards *Brahman*, these, too, comprise a summary of various *Bhagavad Gītā* sections, and especially Chapters 4 and 6. The highest stage of arriving at the supreme abode, both in this life and in the next, is to a large extent a summary of Chapters 7 and 9. This section well exemplifies how *dharmic* duty is gradually sublimated and ultimately turns into devotional service unto the Supreme Person.

You will Fight Anyway

> 57 Just depend upon me in all activities,[23] holding me to be the Supreme; taking refuge in the *yoga* of enlightenment, be constantly absorbed in me 58 Absorbed in me you shall overcome all hardships by my grace. If, however, being under the influence of the ego you will not listen, you will be lost. 59 If, overcome by your ego you would think 'I shall not fight', this resolution would prove in vain, as your own nature will compel you to do so. 60 O Kaunteya, bound by the qualities of work emanating from your own nature, you will be doing helplessly that which you try to avoid out of illusion.

Commentary

Having briefly summarized the *Bhagavad Gītā* in the previous section, Kṛṣṇa's tone becomes more personal, and he calls Arjuna to depend upon him, or to mentally relinquish all his activities unto him. This idea has been previously presented[24] and it seems that now, at the *Bhagavad Gītā's* culmination, Kṛṣṇa invites Arjuna to receive his personal grace, thereby transcending the *guṇas* and overcoming all obstacles on the difficult path to liberation. Kṛṣṇa addresses the hindrance to dependence upon him, and that is the ego which may prevent Arjuna from receiving this advice. Having said that, Kṛṣṇa points at Arjuna's nature which will compel him to fight; it has been previously stated that activity is forced upon

---

20 18.45–48.

21 18.49–53.

22 18.54–56.

23 Literally 'mentally relinquish all activities unto me'.

24 See *BG* 3.30, 8.7 and 9.27.

the embodied soul,[25] and that this activity springs from one's nature.[26] Arjuna will be compelled to act, and as his nature is the nature of a warrior, it will compel him to fight rather than teach, farm or serve. As such, Kṛṣṇa's argument is that it is better to fight for his cause, and thereby receive his grace and attain liberation from *saṁsāra* as well as his supreme abode, than neglecting to hear his advice out of egotism, and consequently finding himself fighting for some other cause which will further entangle him in rebirth. In the next section Kṛṣṇa resorts to an even more personal tone, and as such it comprises to a large extent the *Bhagavad Gītā*'s peak.

Relinquish Everything and Take Refuge in Me Alone

> 61 The Lord abides in the heart of all living beings, O Arjuna, who are mounted on a machine-like apparatus, and he causes them to wander by his magical power. 62 O Bhārata, take refuge in him with all your heart and soul! By his grace you shall attain supreme peace and the eternal abode. 63 Thus have I propounded to you knowledge, the mystery of mysteries; reflect upon it profoundly and then do as you wish. 64 Hear again my supreme message, the highest secret of all; it is your welfare which I have in mind as you are truly dear to me. 65 Always think of me, become my devotee, worship me and pay your homage unto me, and thus you shall undoubtedly come to me; I promise you this as you are dear to me. 66 Abandon all *dharmas* and take refuge in me alone, and I shall release you from all evils; do not fear.

Commentary

The section first offers a brief summary of Chapter 13; it mentions the personal divinity in the heart and the complex relations of the living entity with nature. The present description has a somewhat more personal tone in that it emphasizes the Supreme Person's involvement through his magical nature, as well as a call for Arjuna to take refuge in the supreme with heart and soul. The discourse turns even more personal, and Kṛṣṇa now addresses Arjuna as a friend to his friend, as opposed to the supreme formally addressing a conditioned soul.[27] Kṛṣṇa first asks Arjuna to consider what has been said, and to act as he sees fit; it appears that the full surrender offered is considered as such only when done out of free will, in full reason, knowledge and understanding of the worldview presented by Kṛṣṇa throughout the *Bhagavad Gītā*. Before pronouncing the two central verses of the entire treatise, Kṛṣṇa openly expresses his affection towards Arjuna and beseeches him to pay careful attention to his words for his own good. He then makes the first

---

25 *BG* 3.5 and 18.11.

26 *BG* 18.41.

27 The peak of the formal tone has been exemplified in Chapter 11.

declaration which is almost a replica of Chapter 9's summarizing verse, asking Arjuna to become his devotee, worship him and pay his homage unto him; Kṛṣṇa promises Arjuna that as a result he shall reach him.[28] Following that Kṛṣṇa makes the famous declaration known traditionally as the *carama śloka*;[29] he extends the appeal for devotion by asking Arjuna to reject all *dharmas*, and just take shelter of him alone. Kṛṣṇa assures Arjuna that by doing so, he will release him from all evils. Kṛṣṇa now suggests that Arjuna rejects the various paths which he himself has offered throughout the *Bhagavad Gītā*; Arjuna should simply surrender himself completely unto him, and Kṛṣṇa in turn will release Arjuna from all evils. This devotional ending of the *Bhagavad Gītā* offers a solution to one of the treatise's most difficult problems, i.e. the problem of evil. The solution offered is that by surrendering to Kṛṣṇa in a devotional mood, Kṛṣṇa will personally release Arjuna from all evils, and consequently award him liberation in his proximity. Here ends the dialogue between the two friends, and the next section deals with teaching and disseminating the *Bhagavad Gītā* to others.

Propounding the Message to Others, and Arjuna's Summary

> 67 Never shall this be spoken to one who is not austere and not devoted to me,
> to one who desires not to hear this, or to one who speaks evil of me. 68 One
> who explains this supreme secret to my devotees, thus performing the highest
> devotional service unto me, shall undoubtedly come to me. 69 There is none
> among humans performing a task dearer to me than this, and there shall never
> be on earth one dearer than him to me. 70 And I deem that one who studies and
> recites this, our sacred dialogue, will be worshiping me through the knowledge-
> sacrifice. 71 And one who hears this faithfully and without envy, he too will attain
> liberation and reach the auspicious worlds of those of pious deeds. 72 O Pārtha,
> have you heard this with full concentration? Has your ignorance disappeared
> and your delusion been dispelled, O Dhanañjaya? 73 Arjuna said: By your grace,
> O Acyuta, my illusion is gone and I have recovered my wits; I stand firm and
> free from doubts, and I shall do as you say.

Commentary

Kṛṣṇa now refers to the *Bhagavad Gītā* as a whole; it is to be heard only by austere and devotional persons who desire to hear it, and not by those hostile to the supreme. Those who will disseminate it will attain the highest devotion unto the Supreme Person, will become very dear to him and shall reach him beyond doubt. Whoever teaches or recites this discourse will be worshiping the supreme through the sacrifice of knowledge, and will naturally gain the pious fruits of this offering.

[28] *BG* 18.65 and 9.34.

[29] *BG* 18.66. *Carama śloka*: the final or ultimate verse.

Now it is Arjuna's time to sum up; in reply to Kṛṣṇa's question, Arjuna declares that he has understood Kṛṣṇa's words, has accepted them, and is now about to act according to Kṛṣṇa's instructions and fight. In order to testify that Arjuna declares: '*kariṣye vacanaṁ tava*' – 'I shall do as you say'. Here ends the conversation between Kṛṣṇa and Arjuna, along with its internal summary as well as its second order summary. As the entire treatise was spoken by Sañjaya to Dhṛtarāṣṭra in reply to the king's question,[30] now comes the time for his summary.

Sañjaya's Conclusion – Pāṇḍu's Sons will Emerge Victorious

> 74 Sañjaya said: Thus have I heard the conversation of Vāsudeva and the great soul Pārtha, so astounding that my hair stands on end. 75 By the grace of Vyāsa I have heard this supreme secret of *yoga* directly from Kṛṣṇa, the master of *yoga*, who spoke it personally. 76 O king, reflecting again and again on this wondrous and virtuous colloquy of Keśava and Arjuna, I am thrilled and rejoice again and again. 77 O king, recalling again and again the astonishing form of Hari, my amazement is immense, and joy excites me again and once again. 78 Wherever there is Kṛṣṇa, the master of *yoga*, and wherever there is Pārtha, the carrier of the bow, there will surely be fortune, victory, prosperity and justice. That I verily believe.

Commentary

Sañjaya now sums up his own experience of directly hearing and reciting the *Bhagavad Gītā*; he is experiencing a state of deep amazement, joy and bliss. His conclusion is that victory is certain for Pāṇḍu's sons, since wherever there is Kṛṣṇa and Arjuna, there will certainly be fortune, victory, prosperity and justice.

Thus ends the *Bhagavad Gītā.*

[30] The question opened the *Bhagavad Gītā*: see *BG* 1.1.

Glossary

ācārya	teacher, preceptor
Acyuta	a name of Kṛṣṇa meaning infallible
adharma	that which is contrary to *dharma,* improper, immoral, unlawful
adhikāra	eligibility, qualification
Adhokṣaja	name of both Viṣṇu and Kṛṣṇa meaning 'beyond sense perception'
Ādityas	the 12 gods who are sons of Aditi and their descendants
advaita	non-dual
Advaita Vedānta	a non-dual *Vedānta* school whose famous exponent is Śaṅkara
ahaṅkāra	lit. 'I am the doer'; ego, self-consciousness, the eighth element
Airāvata	a white elephant with four tusks who carries Indra, king of heaven
ajñāna	ignorance, absence of knowledge
ākāśa	ether, the fifth great element
ānanda	bliss, one of the three qualities of *Brahman*
anitya	finite, temporary, non-eternal
apauruṣeya	knowledge received from non-human sources; *śruti* or the *Veda*
Arjuna	son of Paṇḍu and Kuntī, fathered by the god Indra, the third of the five Pāṇḍava brothers, and commander of the Pāṇḍava army, who heard the *Bhagavad Gītā* directly from Kṛṣṇa
āryan	a civilized, refined and noble follower of *Vedic* culture
Asita	presumably a *yogācāry* and father of the sage Devala
āśrama	one of the two categories of *dharma*, which defines one's personal stage of life in terms of *brahmācarya*, *gṛhastha*, *vānaprastha* and *sannyāsa*
aṣṭāṅga yoga	a ladder-like *yoga* system of eight limbs or stages
āstika	traditions conforming to *śruti* or the *Veda* such as the six orthodox *darśanas*
asuras	demons, the opponents of the *devas*, the demonic enemies of the gods; they reside lower than the earth, constantly aspire to dominate the universe, and are influenced by *tamas*, the *guṇa* of darkness
Aśvattha	a sacred tree, presumably the holy Bengali Ficus
Aśvatthāman	son of Droṇa

Aśvins	celestial physicians who made the old sage Cyavana resume his youth; fathered the youngest Pāṇḍavas, Nakula and Sahadeva
ātman	the conscious and eternal self, the spiritual soul
avatāra	divine descent, the Supreme Person appearing in this world in a human or a non-human form
avidyā	absence of knowledge, ignorance
avyakta	undifferentiated *prakṛti* in a primordial state prior to the creation
bandha	bondage to repeated births and deaths
Bhagavad Gītā	lit. 'the Supreme Person's sacred poetical treatise'
bhagavān	the Supreme Person
bhakta	devotee
bhakti	devotion
bhakti yoga	a path leading to *mokṣa* wherein the devotional practices become *yogic* practices
Bhṛgu	a son of Brahmā and a great sage; he was once sent by the sages to find out who is the greatest of the three main gods – Brahmā, Viṣṇu and Śiva, and concluded that Viṣṇu was the greatest
Bhīma	also Bhīmasena; son of Paṇḍu and Kuntī, fathered by the wind god
Bhīṣma	son of Śantanu and Gaṅgā (the river Ganges), a great warrior and the grandsire of the Kuru house
Bhuriṣravas	son of Somadatta
Brahmā	a *Vedic* god, the creator of the universe whose planet is the highest in the universe
brahma jñāna	knowledge of *Brahman*
Brahmacārī	a celibate student who studies under the *guru* and practices various types of austerities
brahmacarya	the first stage in the *āśrama* system, wherein the celibate student studies under the *guru*
Brahman	the Supreme Absolute, characterized by eternity, consciousness and bliss
Brahmasūtra	also called *Vedānta Sūtra*; one of the three founding texts of the *Vedānta* tradition, along with the *Upaniṣads* and the *Bhagavad Gītā*. Comprised of 550 aphorisms summarizing the contents of the *Upaniṣads*
brahmin	(Skt.: *brāhmaṇa*), the priestly and intellectual class, the highest of the four *varṇas*
Bṛhaspati	a celestial sage who served as the priest of the gods; when Indra ignored him out of pride, he disappeared leaving Indra to be defeated by the demons headed by Bali
bṛhatsāma	a chant of the *Sāma Veda samhitā*

buddhi	intellect, one of the 24 elements of *prakṛti*
cakra	a discus used by Kṛṣṇa and Viṣṇu as a weapon
cāṇḍāla	outcaste, a class lower than the *śūdra*
Cekitāna	a *Vṛṣni* warrior
cit	knowledge, consciousness; one of the three qualities of *Brahman*
Citraratha	lord of the *Gandharvas*, served as a calf when the *Gandharvas* milked the earth
daityas	the demons, sons of Diti
darśana	a vision of the truth, one of the six orthodox philosophical schools
deha	the physical body
Devala	a seer and knower of *Brahman* who cursed Hūhū to become a crocodile; it may also be a different seer by that name who is the best of the Śāṇḍilyas, or the son of the *śveta avatāra* of Viṣṇu
Dharma	the god of justice; fathered Yudhiṣṭhira
dharma	a universal principle representing religion, law, order, duty, justice and morality; it upholds the world by categorizing human society into *varṇas* and *āśramas*
Dharmarāja	an epithet of Yudhiṣṭhira meaning king of *dharma*
Dhṛṣṭadyumna	son of Drupada, born from a sacrifice
Dhṛṣṭaketu	king of *Cedi*
Dhṛtarāṣṭra	Paṇḍu's brother, the blind king who was too weak to restrain his greedy and immoral son Duryodhana
Draupadī	daughter of Drupada, sister of Dhṛṣṭadyumna and wife of the five Pāṇḍava brothers
Droṇa	the royal martial arts teacher, who trained both the Pāṇḍavas and the Kauravas in military arts
Drupada	father of Draupadī and Dhṛṣṭadyumna
Duryodhana	eldest son of Dhṛtarāṣṭra, the leader of the Kaurava camp, who was always envious of the Pāṇḍava brothers
dvandva	a word compound in which both components carries the same syntactic weight
dvija	twice-born, a term referring to the members of the three upper *varṇas*, who are considered to be born for the second time through the *upanayana* or initiation rite
ethical ladder	a ladder of various grades of action leading from a mode of action motivated by utilitarianism all the way to a spiritually motivated action; this ladder is at the heart of the *Bhagavad Gītā*'s structure
gandharvas	semi-divine beings endowed with extraordinary personal beauty

Ganges	Skt.: Gaṅgā, a celestial river brought to the earth which now flows down from the Himalayas through India; also known by the name Jāhnavī
Garuḍa	the eagle carrier of Viṣṇu, son of Kaśyapa and Vinatā
gāyatrī	a poetic meter
gṛhastha	the second stage in the *āśrama* system, wherein the celibate student becomes a householder
guru	a teacher or *ācārya* who transmits spiritual wisdom
guṇas	the three subtle qualities of *prakṛti* or material nature; these are *sattva* or goodness, *rajas* or passion and *tamas* or ignorance
Hanumān	the monkey god, servant of Rāma, who appeared on Arjuna's flag
Hierarchical reality	a concept according to which reality is divided into layers and as such is not unified rather is divided
Indra	the king of the heaven and the rain god; has a thousand eyes
itihāsa	'so has it been', a traditional term for history denoting the two great epics, the *Mahābhārata* and the *Rāmāyaṇa*
japa	the sacrifice of muttered prayer; a personal meditation which is performed by repeating a *mantra* directed at one's favoured deity
Jayadratha	king of Sindhu, son in law of Dhṛtarāṣṭra
jīva	the individual soul, the *ātman*
jñāna	knowledge and specifically spiritual knowledge
jñāna yoga	a path leading to *mokṣa* wherein philosophizing and intellectual engagement with the scriptures become *yogic* practices
Kali yuga	according to *purāṇic* accounts, it is the present age of quarrel where *dharma* declines and so are the good qualities of the human being
kalpa	one day of Brahmā
kāma	sensual pleasures, one of the four goals of human life known as *puruṣārthas*
Kāmadhenu	a wish-fulfilling cow; the cow of the sage Jamadagni providing unlimited milk
Kandarpa	god of love
Kapila	an *avatāra* of Viṣṇu, born to Kardama and Devahūti, who propounded the knowledge of Sāṅkhya
karma	action and its various implications in future lives
karma indriyas	the five organs of action; voice, hands, legs, the excretion and procreation organs
karma yoga	a path leading to *mokṣa* wherein action according to *dharma* becomes a *yogic* practice

Karṇa	son of Kuntī by the Sun god, before her marriage to Paṇḍu; he was abandoned and adopted by a couple of a low social status, and thereby deprived of his royal status; was Arjuna's main rival, although Arjuna never knew that they were brothers; promised his mother, Kuntī, that she would be left with five sons after the battle, meaning that either he or Arjuna would be killed
Kṛpa	teacher of the Kauravas
Kṛṣṇa	the speaker of the *Bhagavad Gītā*, the Supreme Person appearing in this world to uphold *dharma*, Arjuna's friend and cousin who offered Arjuna to serve as his chariot driver during the great war
kṣatriya	the warrior and ruling class comprised of nobles and royals
Kuntī	Pāṇḍu's wife and the mother of the three elder Pāṇḍava brothers, Yuddhiṣṭhira, Bhīma and Arjuna
Kuntibhoja	foster father of Kuntī
Kuvera	the lord of wealth and king of the underworld, resembles the Greek Pluto; Lord of Yakṣas and brother of Śiva
līlā	divine play, a spiritual mode of action free from any utilitarian purpose
Mahābhārata	the great Sanskrit epic depicting the story of the Kuru house, which includes the *Bhagavad Gītā*
makara	a sea monster; different translators have rendered the term as a crocodile, a shark and a leviathan
manas	mind
Manu	the son of Brahmā and the father of the human race; one of the authorities on *dharma* and compiler of a *dharma śāstra* called the *manu smṛti*
Mārgaśīrṣa	the first month according to the *Vedic* calendar; takes place during February–March
Marīci	a son of Brahmā born along with Nārada at the beginning of the creation, and father of Kaśyapa; directed Indra's horse sacrifice and punished the demonic king Vena by cursing him
Maruts	49 gods who are sons of Kaśyapa and Diti; brothers of Indra
māyā	illusion
Meru	an enormous celestial mountain situated at the middle of the world, somewhere between the sun and the earth
mokṣa	liberation from the cycle of rebirth
Nakula and Sahadeva	sons of Paṇḍu by his wife Madrī; fathered by the celestial physicians called Aśvins

Nārada	son of Brahmā who was taught the divine wisdom known as the *Bhāgavata* by his father, and who passed it on to his great disciple Vyāsa; travels through the universe while praising the Supreme Person with his *vīṇā* (a musical instument), is one of the 12 authorities on *dharma* and compiler of the *Nārada bhaktisūtra* which is a treatise on devotion
nāstika	traditions not conforming to *śruti* or the *Veda* such as Buddhism and Jainism
nirguṇa	devoid of attributes
nirvāṇa	extinction of material existence
niṣkāma karma	acting while disinterested in action's fruits, a central teaching of the *Bhagavad Gītā*
pañca bhūtas	the five great elements – earth, water, fire, air and ether
pañca tanmātras	five sense objects – sound, touch, form, taste and smell
Pāṇḍava brothers	the five brothers, sons of Paṇḍu and heroes of the *Mahābhārata*: Yudhiṣṭhira, Bhīma, Arjuna, Nakula and Sahadeva
Paṇḍu	Born of the divine sage Vyāsa, Dhṛtarāṣṭra's younger brother, the father of the five Pāṇḍava brothers, and the rightful king of the empire. As a result of a curse, he was not able to conceive children, and therefore his wives, Kuntī and Madrī, called upon five different gods to father
pāpa	evil, bad karma, sin
paramārtha	the highest, absolute reality
paramparā	disciplic succession, a continuous chain of *gurus* and disciples
Prahlāda	the son of the demonic king Hiraṇyakaśipu; although born in a demonic family, he was one of the greatest devotees of Viṣṇu, so much so, that Viṣṇu appeared as the Lion-Man *avatāra* to rescue him from his demonic father
prakṛti	material nature consisting of the three *guṇas*
pralaya	the universal destruction
pramāṇa	means of valid knowledge
prasāda	divine grace
prasthānatraya	the three foundations of the *Vedānta* tradition; the *Bhagavad Gītā*, the *Brahma Sūtras* and the *Upaniṣads*
puṇya	meritorious *karma*
Purojit	another name for Kuntibhoja, the foster father of Kuntī
puruṣa	the Supreme Person. See 8.8, 8.10, 8.22, 15.4, 15.18–19
puruṣārthas	the four goals of human life; *dharma*, *artha*, *kāma* and *mokṣa*
rajas	one of the three *guṇas* representing passion, desire, attachment to the fruits of action and excessive endeavours

rākṣasas	evil spirits who are semi-divine beings
Rāma	an *avatāra* of Viṣṇu and hero of the great epos Rāmāyaṇa, who rescued his saintly wife Sītā from the demon Rāvaṇa; this may also refer to Paraśurāma (Rāma who carries the axe), an *avatāra* of Viṣṇu, and who killed 21 generations of kings
Rāmāyaṇa	the great Sanskrit epic depicting the story of Rāma
Rudras	a group of 11 gods worshipped for the attainment of power
Sādhyas	the 12 celestial sons of Dharma and Sādhya
saguṇa	with attributes
samādhi	the peak of the *yoga* practice, an introverted state of spiritual realization
Sāma Veda	the most musical of the four Vedas
saṁsāra	the chain of repeated births and deaths, the state of worldly existence
Sañjaya	Dhṛtarāṣṭra's secretary who described the battle to him
Sāṅkhya	one of the six orthodox philosophical traditions, propounding the differentiation of *prakṛti* from the *puruṣa*
Sannyāsa	the fourth and last stage of the *āśrama* system, the stage of renunciation
Sannyāsī	a person in the fourth and highest stage of the *āśrama* system, a renounced celibate and generally wandering ascetic
śāstra	the traditional authoritative teachings
Sattva	one of the three *guṇas* representing purity, serenity, goodness and knowledge
Satyaki	a famous Yādava warrior and a friend of Kṛṣṇa
Śiva	the great god, one of the three main universal deities along with Brahmā and Viṣṇu and who is considered the Supreme according to Śaivism; he is in charge of the *tamo guṇa*, and is therefore endowed with the task of destroying the universe when the time for annihilation comes; is an ascetic and lives in mount Kailāsa
Siddhas	celestial beings who are endowed with various mystic powers
Skanda	son of Śiva and god of war
smṛti	a category of humanly authored canonical texts such as the epics and the *purānas*
Son of Subhadrā	Abhimanyu; son of Arjuna and Subhadrā
Sons of Draupadī	five sons fathered by each of the five Pāṇḍava brothers
Soteriology	doctrines of salvation
śruti	a category of non-humanly revealed canonical text, such as the *Vedas* and the *Upaniṣads*
Subhadrā	sister of Kṛṣṇa, wife of Arjuna, mother of Abhimanyu
śūdra	the serving class comprised of serfs, menial workers and artisans

sūtra	a short and condensed aphorism, conveying knowledge
svarga	heaven, eden
tamas	one of the three *guṇas* representing darkness, ignorance, illusion and indolence
Uccaiḥśravas	a horse born through the churning of the ocean of milk by the gods and demons
upanayana	initiation rite
Upaniṣads	late *Vedic* philosophical texts propounding the unity of *ātman* and *Brahman*
Uttamaujas	a pañcala prince who was an especially great warrior
vaikuṇṭha	the abode of Viṣṇu which is eternal, spiritual, pure and beyond the influence of the three *guṇas*
vaiṣṇava	a devotee of Viṣṇu
vaiśya	the merchant and agricultural class
vānaprastha	the third stage of the *āśrama* system, a forest-dweller
varṇa	class system, category; refers to the four social classes of *brāhmaṇas*, *kṣatriyas*, *vaiṣyas* and *śūdras*
varṇāśrama dharma	duty according to one's specific *varṇa* and *āśrama*, the basic *Vedic* social structure
Varuṇa	Lord of the oceans who resides therein, King of the *asuras*
Vāsudeva	Kṛṣṇa, the speaker of the *Bhagavad Gītā*, son of Vasudeva and Devakī
Vasus	a group of eight gods who are sons of Dharma and Vasu; they were cursed to be born on the earth, but then returned to heaven. Seven of them returned immediately whereas the eighth lived on earth for a full life span. This was Bhīṣma, the grandfather of the Kuru dynasty who participated in the Kurukṣetra battle as the Kauravas' commander-in-chief
Vedānta	'the end of knowledge', the orthodox school of philosophy derived from the *Bhagavad Gītā*, *Brahma Sūtras* and the *Upaniṣads*
Vikarṇa	a son of Dhṛtarāṣṭra
Virāṭa	a king who sheltered the Pāṇḍava brothers while they were in exile
Viṣṇu	the great god whose abode called Vaikuṇṭha is far beyond this universe, and who is identified in the *Bhagavad Gītā* with Kṛṣṇa; appears in his *avatāra* form whenever and wherever there is a decline of *dharma* and a rise of *adharma*, is considered the Supreme Person according to *Vaiṣṇavism*
Vṛṣni	the dynasty in which Kṛṣṇa was born

Vyāsa	the author of the *Mahābhārata,* who divided the Veda into four
vyavahāra	empirical reality
yajña	sacrifice, and in particular a *Vedic* sacrifice
Yakṣas	a semi-celestial group of the demon class, followers of Śiva, headed by Kuvera
Yama	Lord of death; resides in the lower regions of the universe and punishes humans after death according to their deeds; is an authority on *dharma*
Yoga	one of the six orthodox *darśanas*, offering a disciplined path aiming at the state of *samādhi*
yoga-sūtra	a classical text traditionally ascribed to Patañjali, propounding the *aṣṭāṅga yoga* system
Yudhamanyu	a Pañcala prince
Yudhiṣṭhira	the eldest Pāṇḍava brother and their leader
yugas	universal ages; *kṛta*, *tretā*, *dvāpara* and *kali*
Yuyudhana	another name for Satyaki

Bibliography

Bhūrijana Dāsa, *Surrender Unto Me*, VIHE Publications, New Delhi, 1997.

Biderman, S., *Indian Philosophy – The Foundations*, Broadcast University Press, Tel Aviv, 1980.

Dikshitar, V.R.R. (ed.), *The Purāṇa Index*, Madras University Historical Series, no. 15, The University of Madras, Madras, 1951.

Edgerton, F., *The Bhagavad Gītā*, Harvard University Press, Cambridge, MA, 1972 (originally published 1964).

Klostermaier, K.K., *A Survey of Hinduism*, 2nd edition, SUNY, Albany, 1994.

__________, *A Concise Encyclopedia of Hinduism*, Oneworld, Oxford, 1998.

Olivelle, P., *Upaniṣads*, Oxford University Press, Oxford, 1996.

Raghavacar, S.S., *Rāmānuja on the Gītā*, Advaita Ashrama – Rāmakṛṣṇa Vedānta Centre, Calcutta, 1991.

Rāmānuja, *Śrī Rāmānuja Gītā Bhāṣya*, translated by Ādidevānanda Svāmī, Śrī Rāmakṛṣṇa Math, Madras, 1991.

Śaṅkarācārya, *The Bhagavad Gītā With The Commentary of Ādi Śrī Śaṅkarācārya*, translated by A.M. Śāstri, Samata Books, Chennai, 1995 (originally published 1897).

Sharma, A., *The Hindu Gītā*, Duckworth, London, 1986.

Van Buitenen, J.A.B., *The Bhagavadgītā in the Mahābhārata*, The University of Chicago Press, Chicago and London, 1981.

__________, 'A Contribution to the Critical Edition of the *Bhagavad gītā*', *Studies in Indian Literature and Philosophy*, Motilal Banarsidas, Delhi, 1988 (originally published in the *Journal of the American Oriental Society*, 86, 1966, pp. 99–109).

Zaehner, R.C., *The Bhagavad-Gītā*, Oxford University Press, Oxford, 1969.

Index